GOD IS
MY REFUGE

GOD IS MY REFUGE

12 WEEKS OF DEVOTIONS AND SCRIPTURE MEMORY FOR TROUBLED TIMES

KATHY HOWARD

GOD IS MY REFUGE

12 Weeks of Devotions and Scripture Memory for Troubled Times

ISBN 978-0-89112-330-9
LCCN 2012037283

Printed in the United States of America

LIBRARY OF CONGRESS CATALOGING-IN-PUBLICATION DATA
Howard, Kathy, 1961-
God is my refuge : twelve weeks of devotions and scripture memory for troubled times / Kathy Howard.
p. cm.
ISBN 978-0-89112-330-9
1. Devotional literature. I. Title.
BV4832.3.H69 2013
242'.4--dc23

2012037283

Cover design by Elizabeth Fulton
Interior text design by Sandy Armstrong

Leafwood Publishers is an imprint of
Abilene Christian University Press
1626 Campus Court
Abilene, Texas 79601

1-877-816-4455
www.leafwoodpublishers.com

13 14 15 16 17 18 / 7 6 5 4 3 2 1

To my great God and Savior.

You have been my refuge during dark days.
May you be forever praised.

Contents

Acknowledgments

Isn't it just like God? Not long after I began working on this book, our family entered a time of crisis. I praise and thank my God, who has indeed been our refuge—and an ever-present help in our time of trouble.

I also want to thank the dear Christian friends and prayer partners who have surrounded us during these days: Connie, Janet, Lee, Kelly, Lisa, Jan, Susan, and Cathy.

You are precious.

Introduction

Are you in the middle of an overwhelming situation? Have you recently experienced a loss? Are you or a family member facing an illness, job loss, or personal crisis? Are you just struggling with life in general?

God sees. He knows all about your circumstances. And He cares. *Cast all your anxiety on him because he cares for you* (1 Pet. 5:7). He invites you to come to Him with all of it. *Cast your cares on the LORD and he will sustain you; he will never let the righteous fall* (Ps. 55:22). He desires to be your help and strength. *God is our refuge and strength, an ever-present help in trouble* (Ps. 46:1).

This devotional book is designed to help you bring your cares to God so you can experience what only He can provide. He wants to comfort you in your grief, give you hope in times of discouragement, and fill you with joy in seasons of sadness.

Over the next twelve weeks, immerse yourself in the promises of God's Word. Each week focuses on a different challenge that life may throw your way, from material needs and illness to broken relationships and loss. Through the five days of devotions each week, you will experience God's heart for you in the midst of that struggle.

The first devotion of each week highlights a verse for you to memorize. (I memorize from the *New International Version*, but you use the translation you like best.) I strongly encourage you to accept the challenge of memorizing these twelve Scriptures over the course of this book. Memorizing God's Word solidly entrenches His truth in your heart and mind. Then, through it,

God can minister to you in powerful and very personal ways. Here are just a few ways God can work in your life through His Word:

- Provide you with comfort, encouragement, peace, and strength (Col. 3:15–16; Ps. 1:1–3).
- Give you guidance and wisdom (Ps. 37:31; Ps. 119:24, 98, 105).
- Foster your spiritual growth (2 Tim. 3:16–17; Heb. 4:12; 1 Pet. 2:2).
- Prepare you to share your faith with others (1 Pet. 3:15; Acts 18:28).
- Fill you with joy and pour out His blessings (Ps. 119:24, 47, 103; James 1:21–25).

The thought of memorizing Scripture is overwhelming for many Christians—me included! That's why this devotional gives you daily, doable steps to help you succeed. You can do it, and the effort is more than worth it. God will use His Word in your life to care for you.

Note: One thing you should have ready in advance is a way to record and store your memory verses. Here are a few suggestions:

- Index cards and a recipe box.
- Blank cards the size of business cards and a business card file. (These files look a bit like small photo albums and come in various sizes.)
- Card stock cut to fit a photo album with plastic sleeves. (You can cut your paper the right size: 4x6 or 5x7.) Also, if you need additional space, consider keeping a journal or notebook to write your responses to the reflection questions or to record

your prayers each day. You may find great blessings in being able to look back and see how God has worked in your life and heart over the weeks of this devotional.

WEEK ONE

TROUBLE

Memory Verse

God is our refuge and strength,
an ever-present help in trouble.

Psalm 46:1

Day One

A Safe Place

Read: Psalm 46:1–7
Weekly memory verse: Psalm 46:1

"Safe! I'm on base. I'm safe! You can't get me now!"

Remember playing the game of tag as a child? The person who was "it" chased all the other players, hoping to tag one and make them "it" for the next round. Most of the players ran quickly to the safety of home base. However, at least one player would usually tempt fate by continuing to run around, barely darting out of the grasp of "it" again and again. Not me, though. I always ran straight to home base and the protection it provided.

I haven't played tag in a very long time, but I still need a safe place to run to when the troubles of life threaten to overtake me. I need a refuge—a shelter, a place of safety that protects me from danger and trouble.

In John 16:33, Jesus said His followers *will* have trouble in this world. We live in a fallen world, full of troubles of all kinds. In fact, sometimes, like the mountains in Psalm 46:3, we may see our lives crumbling around us while the flood waters rise. But God offers protection for His children in distress.

According to Psalm 46:1, God is our refuge, our "ever-present help in trouble." He has the power to save and the authority to act. We don't have to fear our circumstances. God is bigger than our personal crisis, any physical disaster, or any political upheaval. Whenever and wherever His children need help, God is there.

Reflect and Apply

What troubles, difficulties, or heartaches are you dealing with now?

List the things you learned about God from today's Scripture.

Do you believe God is bigger than your troubles? Reflect on how God may choose to use your troubles for His purposes.

Prayer Prompt

Write a prayer to God, acknowledging Him as your refuge, your place of safety.

Memory Minute

Each day of devotions will guide you through a quick exercise to help you memorize that week's memory verse. Please take a minute or two each day to follow the suggestions, and by the end of the week you should know it "by heart." Don't forget to review your memorized verses regularly.

For a constant reminder that God is our source of strength and place of safety, commit to memorize Psalm 46:1.

1. Read the verse.
2. Read the verses immediately surrounding it to understand the context in which it is written (in this case, read Psalm 46:1–3).

3. Rewrite the verse in your own words at the bottom of this page (or in your journal).
4. Write the verse and reference on a card. This card should fit the type of storage system you've chosen for your verses. (See the note at the end of the Introduction for suggestions.)
5. Read it out loud three times.

Day Two

God Hears

Read: Psalm 116:1–5
Weekly memory verse: Psalm 46:1

When our three children were little, my husband, Wayne, could sleep even if one of them was in the bed with us, crying in the aftermath of a nightmare. But all it took for me to pop up in bed awake was one small whimper from across the house. If one child went to bed not feeling well, I slept poorly that night. I would only doze off and on, anticipating being needed. It seemed my mom ears were constantly listening for my children's calls.

Overwhelmed with trouble, the author of Psalm 116 called out to God for help. God heard and acted. God saved him and met his needs. The psalmist responded to God's attentive care with praise and a declaration of love. Now that the psalmist has experienced God's faithfulness, he will continue to call upon the one God who is willing and able to save.

Our heavenly Father hears the cries of His children. His ears are turned our direction, anticipating our needs, longing to hear us call His name. And when our cries for help reach His ears, He moves to save us. He acts on our behalf because He is gracious, righteous, and compassionate. God helps His children when they put their faith and trust in the only One who is able to save them from all their troubles. Who do you trust to call when faced with trouble?

Reflect and Apply

Where do you usually turn first when you are troubled or distressed? Do you turn to God or to a friend, spouse, thing, or activity?

Do you believe God hears your cries for help? Do you believe He is able to help?

If God hears our cries and is able to act, why do you think we might turn first to some place or someone other than to God?

Prayer Prompt

Cry out to God now. Lay all your hurts and needs before Him in prayer.

Memory Minute

1. Read Psalm 46:1 from the card you created yesterday.
2. Spend a moment thinking about what this verse teaches about the following:

    - What you should believe about God.
    - Things you can praise or thank God for.
    - What you can pray for yourself or others.

3. Identify two to four key words or "anchor" words in the verse to help you remember it. For instance, in Psalm 46:1, three solid anchor words to remember could be *refuge*, *strength*, and *help*. Circle these words on the front of the card and then write them on the back.

4. Recite the verse three times. The first time, read it from the card. The second time, check the anchor words on the front and then recite it. The third time, turn the card over and try to recite it by only looking at the anchor words.

Day Three

God Our Savior

Read: Isaiah 43:1–4
Weekly memory verse: Psalm 46:1

My mother once saved my life. When I was about four years old, I fell in a lake and didn't know how to swim. By the time Mom got to the edge of the water, I was quite a ways from the shore and going under yet again. She dove in and quickly brought me safely to dry ground.

God saved His people Israel. He chose them out of all nations to be His. God rescued them from slavery in Egypt. He brought them safely through the waters of the Red Sea. Then, after centuries of rebellion, the prophet Isaiah warned them of God's pending discipline. They would soon face exile in Babylon, but God would redeem them again. Like a loving father, God would lavish His children with grace and mercy. He would snatch them out of exile and bring them safely home.

God has a unique relationship with us, His people. First, He made us. He intimately formed you and me. Then He chose us to belong to Him. He called us by name. He redeemed us out of slavery to sin and claimed us as His own. He promises to save those who belong to Him.

Are you passing through a fire right now? Whether you're experiencing God's discipline, being persecuted for your faith, or undergoing a refining trial, God is with you. You may feel the heat and smell the smoke, but you will not be consumed. God may not choose to rescue you *out* of every trouble, but He will always rescue you *through* them. He will not leave your side.

Reflect and Apply

God's greatest act of salvation on your behalf was in sending His Son to save you from your sins and give you eternal life. Have you received God's great gift of eternal salvation?

Have you experienced God's saving hand in past circumstances of your life? If so, when?

Remember, the God who saved your soul and acted on your behalf in the past is the same God today. Will you trust Him with your current circumstances?

Prayer Prompt

If you are a Christian, thank God for the eternal salvation you have received through Jesus. Now continue to thank God for other times in your life you have experienced His saving action on your behalf.

Memory Minute

1. Read Psalm 46:1 from the card you wrote on Day One.
2. On the back of the card, draw a symbol or picture that visually represents the verse. For instance, for Psalm 46:1 you could draw a fort or castle.
3. Turn the card facedown so only the anchor words you wrote yesterday and the picture you drew today can be seen. On a

scratch sheet of paper, write out the verse with the reference. Refer to the anchor words and picture if you need help.

4. Now, without looking at either side of the card, recite the verse and reference from memory. Good work! You're almost there.

Day Four

God of All Comfort

Read: 2 Corinthians 1:3–7
Weekly memory verse: Psalm 46:1

I spent some time recently with a friend who is heartbroken over a family situation. We talked a lot and cried together. But we also laughed together. I believe this was possible because I know exactly how she feels. I've been through the same circumstance she's going through now. And since God comforted me in my situation, I could share His comfort with her.

The Apostle Paul calls God the "God of all comfort." Paul ought to know. He faced plenty of hardships in which he needed God's comfort. In chapters 6 and 11 of 2 Corinthians, Paul mentions beatings, imprisonments, hunger, shipwrecks, betrayal, and more. Paul knew the "God of all comfort" because he had experienced that comfort time and time again. Paul experienced peace in the midst of adversity by trusting in God's faithfulness. He had learned to cling to God in troubled times and trust Him completely. Through all this, God prepared and equipped Paul to comfort others.

Have you personally experienced God's comfort in trouble? Have you ever been comforted through a Christian friend? God is the source of *all* comfort, whether it comes directly from Him or indirectly through His people. Whenever God allows suffering in your life, He is also standing by to give you comfort. Trust

God to comfort you. Cling to Him and trust in His faithfulness to comfort.

Reflect and Apply

How has God comforted you in past trials?

Do you know of anyone who would benefit now from the comfort God gave you then? Are you willing to share it with them?

Is there a Christian friend you can talk to who will understand what you're going through now? Will you allow her to comfort you?

Prayer Prompt

Thank God for the times He has comforted you in the past. Ask Him to show you how you can use that experience to help comfort others.

Memory Minute

1. Recite Psalm 46:1 without looking at either the front or back of your card. If you can't get started, sneak a peek at your anchor words.
2. Write the verse out on another card. Put this verse in a prominent place where you will see it multiple times a day, such as your bathroom mirror, the refrigerator, or car dashboard. Every time you notice the card, use it as an opportunity to review the verse.
3. Get creative! Use your own learning style to help you memorize Psalm 46:1. If you are an auditory learner, you could record the verse and play it back or turn the verse into

a song. If you are a physical or tactile learner, pick an object in your home that represents the verse. For instance, you could select a rock or a stone object to remind you that God is a refuge, a strong, safe place.

4. Pray the verse out loud to God, adding your own thoughts and feelings as you pray.

Day Five

Calm in Chaos

Read: John 14:1–4
Weekly memory verse: Psalm 46:1

My husband and I have moved seven times in our twenty-eight years of marriage. We've learned from experience that God uses Wayne's job to move us where He wants us. But the move from Casper, Wyoming, tested our trust more than the others. When the company announced it was closing its office in Casper, many employees were worried about their futures. Some would be moved to another office, some would be encouraged to retire early, and some would lose their jobs. More than a few asked Wayne how he could remain so calm. He simply told them he trusted God to take care of his future.

The night Jesus was betrayed, the disciples were confused and uncertain. The departure Jesus had told them about in the days and weeks leading up to that night was now imminent. The events about to take place would throw them into chaos. But Jesus pointed them to an alternative—"trust in God." The disciples could have calm in the middle of chaos if they trusted in God and His sovereignty. Jesus' death was God's plan of salvation. The trial that would cause them grief, pain, and fear would ultimately bring God's best.

We too can trust God with our present and our future no matter how bleak they look. We can take comfort in the presence of Christ's Spirit with us now and in the promise of an eternity spent with Him. We can be calm in the midst of chaos because we know "God works for the good of those who love him, who have been called according to his purpose" (Rom. 8:28).

Reflect and Apply

How do you usually respond when your life is in chaos?

What does this response reveal about what you believe about God?

Why is God trustworthy when you are facing trouble and difficult circumstances?

Prayer Prompt

Confess to God any disbelief and lack of trust. Ask Him to strengthen your faith in Him and help you to know that He is trustworthy.

Memory Minute

1. On a scratch piece of paper, try writing Psalm 46:1 without looking at your card or your anchor words. If after a moment you still can't get started, then look at the anchor words or the first word only of the verse to get you going.
2. Spend a moment reflecting on the truth of this Scripture. How does God want you to apply this verse to your life today? Is there a truth you need to accept? Is there a decision you need to make? Is there an action you need to take? Is there an attitude you need to change?
3. Pray and commit to do what God revealed to you.
4. Now recite Psalm 46:1 again, like you mean it!

WEEK TWO

NEED

Memory Verse

But seek first his kingdom and his righteousness,
and all these things will be given to you as well.

Matthew 6:33

Day One

How Much More

Read: Matthew 6:25–33
Weekly memory verse: Matthew 6:33

Last week, I bought a small lemon tree and planted it in a beautiful new pot on the patio. I placed it in just the right spot—it will get all the sun it needs, and I can see it from my living room and kitchen. Within hours, a butterfly and a bee found the tree and promptly performed their God-given task. I'm already thinking about how I will use the lemons.

God's concern and care for His creation astound me. He created a tree to produce tart, sweet fruit, and then He developed the system of pollination to make sure the lemons grow. If God cares for a lemon tree enough to send the butterfly and the bee, just imagine how much more He cares about you, His child!

In the Sermon on the Mount, Jesus reminded His audience of God's provision for His creation to ease their worries. Considering God's faithful character can strengthen our faith in His care for us. If God so abundantly and lovingly cares for birds and flowers, how much more will He care for those who are made in His image?

Often, we allow worry to consume our thoughts and energy. But, just like Jesus said, worry doesn't add an hour to our lives or pay the electric bill. We forget that the same God who feeds the sparrow and pollinates the lemon bloom knows our every need.

But if we focus on pursuing God and make His will our priority, He will meet all our needs.

Reflect and Apply

Are you worried now? If so, what consumes your thoughts today?

Take a moment to reflect on the way God cares for His creation. What have you noticed recently that shows God's faithful provision?

Based on what you read in Matthew today, does God care about your needs? How can you know?

Prayer Prompt

Voice your worries to God. Now ask Him to replace your worry with trust in His loving care and faithful provision.

Memory Minute

Commit to memorize Matthew 6:33 as a reminder to stay focused on God, the One who will meet all your needs.

1. Read the verse, Matthew 6:33, in your favorite translation.
2. Rewrite the verse in your own words at the bottom of this page.
3. Write the verse and reference on the same kind of card you used for the first week's memory verse.
4. Read Matthew 6:33 out loud three times.
5. Pull out the memory verse card for Psalm 46:1 and read through it. Now recite it without looking at the card.

Day Two

A Father's Good Gifts

Read: Luke 11:9–13

Weekly memory verse: Matthew 6:33

When I was a girl, I took my parents' provision for granted. I always had enough food to eat and clothes to wear. They provided me with a used car in good working condition when I started my last year of high school. They paid my way through college.

I didn't know—and honestly may not have cared at the time—that my mom and dad went without things they wanted in order to give to me. My mom didn't buy clothes she needed so I could have a prom dress. My parents didn't go on vacation so I could get an education.

I realize not all earthly parents properly care for their children, but that is not the norm. Most parents, even with all their sin and imperfections, respond to their children with kindness and love. Most desire to abundantly provide for them. So how much more will our perfect heavenly Father respond to our petitions with kindness and long to give us good gifts?

Jesus taught His disciples to pray to God as "Father." If you are a believer in Jesus Christ, you have access to God because you are His child. On the basis of this relationship, you can freely bring your needs and requests to Him and He will listen.

Yes, God knows our needs before we ask, but prayer is an expression of relationship. Through it we acknowledge our trust that He can and will provide for our needs. Ask and receive!

Reflect and Apply

Were your earthly parents always sensitive to your physical needs? How does your relationship with them affect the way you view your relationship with your heavenly Father?

Earthly parents can never be perfect, but God is always the perfect parent. What will that look like in the way He cares for you? In the way He provides for your needs?

Describe the freedom you have to bring your needs and requests to God. Will you do that today?

Prayer Prompt

Thank God for His role as your Father. Ask Him to help you better understand the nature of your relationship with Him as His child.

Memory Minute

1. Read Matthew 6:33 from the card you created yesterday.
2. Spend a moment thinking about the truths in this verse:
    - What does it mean to "seek God's kingdom and righteousness?"
    - What would this look like in your day-to-day life?
    - Ask God to help you seek Him first today.

3. Identify two to four anchor words in the verse to help you remember it. Circle these words on the front of the card and then write them on the back.
4. Recite the verse three times. The first time, read it from the card. The second time, check the anchor words on the front and then recite it. The third time, turn the card over and try to recite it by only looking at the anchor words.

Day Three

Lasting Provision

Read: John 6:34–40
Weekly memory verse: Matthew 6:33

A human being really only needs a few basic necessities to stay alive—food, water, clothing, and shelter. Our heavenly Father generously provides these things and more! I'm thankful God chooses to bless us with good things to enrich our lives. However, the lives of American celebrities prove that the "stuff" of this life cannot satisfy our deeper needs.

In spite of their fame and fortune, many celebrities experience one painful situation after another. They possess beauty, fast cars, and big houses, but addiction, depression, and betrayal tarnish their lives. They move in and out of relationships. They get nipped and tucked in an attempt to hang onto something they're afraid to lose. Success and money fail to meet their spiritual longing, but they continue to pursue them.

Our faces may not grace the cover of *People* magazine, but we are still vulnerable to the lure of materialism. Like the crowds that followed Jesus, we are willing to settle for more of the same. They wanted more bread like He miraculously gave them on the mountain the day before. We want faster food, nicer clothes, and a three-car garage. Like them, we fail to accept the spiritual provision Jesus offers.

Like a doting Father, God delights in meeting our physical needs. But He's even more concerned about our spiritual needs. We need bread, but it only has temporary value. Jesus holds spiritual fulfillment and eternal life in His outstretched hand and bids us "come."

Reflect and Apply

Think about times in the past when you finally got some physical thing you longed for. How long did your happiness last? How long was it before you wanted something else?

Honestly consider what you feel is lacking in your life. Can spiritual needs be met by material things or do they require something more?

Do you believe Jesus is able to meet all your needs, both physical and spiritual?

Prayer Prompt

Ask God to show you your spiritual needs and how Jesus can meet them. Then ask Him to quench your spiritual thirst!

Memory Minute

1. Read Matthew 6:33 from the card you wrote on Day One of this week.
2. On the back of the card, draw a symbol or picture that visually represents the verse.
3. Turn the card facedown so that only the anchor words you wrote yesterday and the picture you drew today can be

seen. On a scratch sheet of paper, write out the verse with the reference. Refer to the anchor words and picture if you need help.

4. Now, without looking at either side of the card, recite the verse and reference from memory.
5. Try to quote Psalm 46:1, your memory verse from Week One, without looking at the card. If you need help, look at your anchor words on the back of the card.

Day Four

No Cost Too Great

Read: Romans 8:31–35
Weekly memory verse: Matthew 6:33

We make decisions every day based on cost. "Is it worth the price?" "Will I get a sufficient return on my investment?" "Does the benefit outweigh the cost?" "Can I afford the risk?" We ask these kinds of questions about everything from hamburger meat to marriage proposals to business deals. In the end, what it gets down to is this: Is what I'll gain valuable enough to pay the price?

The greatest need in everyone's life is salvation. We've all sinned (Rom. 3:23), thereby earning the debt of spiritual death—eternal separation from God (Rom. 6:23). Without someone to intervene, without a Savior to pay the price, we all stand condemned (John 3:18).

Our loving Creator desires a relationship with us. He longs to forgive our sin and graciously give us the gift of eternal life. However, the cost is high. God's justice demands the debt be paid. The debt requires a life to be given.

Praise God! While I was sinner, while you were a sinner, Christ died for us. It doesn't matter who or what may be against us in life, because God is for us. Our heavenly Father saw our condition and determined we were worth the cost. If God freely gave even His Son for us, He will also richly provide for all our needs.

Believer, God looked at you and saw your need for a Savior. He counted the cost and offered His Son. He loves you that much.

Reflect and Apply

Do you ever doubt the depth of God's love for you? How much do you think God must love you to give His Son to save you?

Make a brief list of things or people you feel are "against" you. Compare this list to the One who is "for" you. Which side wins?

What is the biggest need you have today? Based on today's Scripture passage, do you think God is willing and able to meet it?

Prayer Prompt

Voice to God the need weighing on your mind today. Ask Him to help you see this need in light of His previous provision—since He gave His Son, He will also meet this need.

Memory Minute

1. Recite Matthew 6:33 without looking at either the front or back of your card. If you can't get started, sneak a peek at your anchor words.
2. Write the verse out on another card. Put this verse in a prominent place where you will see it multiple times a day, such as your bathroom mirror, the refrigerator, or car dashboard. Every time you notice the card, use it as an opportunity to review the verse.
3. Get creative! Use your own learning style to help you memorize Matthew 6:33. If you are an auditory learner, you could

record the verse and play it back or turn the verse into a song. If you are a physical or tactile learner, pick an object in your home that represents the verse.

4. Pray the verse out loud to God, adding your own thoughts and feelings as you pray.

Day Five

Pay It Forward

Read: 2 Corinthians 9:6–11
Weekly memory verse: Matthew 6:33

Pay It Forward, a popular movie produced in 2000, tells the story of Trevor, an eleven-year-old boy from a troubled home. His new social studies teacher gives the class an unusual assignment: develop a practical plan to make the world a better place and then carry it out. Young Trevor takes the assignment seriously.

Trevor put his plan in action by helping three people in a tangible way. Then he asked them to repay his favor by "paying it forward." They were not to help Trevor, but instead to help three others in need. Each of those three should help three more and so on. Individuals whose needs were met in turn met the needs of others. Giving rippled out from Trevor's town, changing lives as it went. The popularity of the movie created new interest in the "pay it forward" concept, but the core truth comes from God.

Paul encouraged the Corinthian church to collect an offering to help the struggling Christians in Jerusalem by reminding them of God's principles for giving and of His generosity to them. God intends for the financial resources, wisdom, experiences, time, and talent He pours into our lives to be shared with others in need. And as we give, God continues to bless us for future giving.

Giving to others shows our gratitude for God's blessings and expresses faith in His future provision. Generous living invites

God's continued grace in our lives so we can fulfill His purposes for us.

Reflect and Apply

Make a quick list of all the ways God has blessed you. Consider financial resources, life experiences, education, time, and more.

How can viewing your resources as God's affect your desire to use them to bless and help others?

Is there a specific need of someone else God has laid on your heart today? If so, how can you "pay it forward" in his or her life?

Prayer Prompt

Ask God to help you see His blessings to you as a resource for blessing others. Ask Him to give you excitement and joy in meeting their needs.

Memory Minute

1. On a scratch piece of paper, try writing Matthew 6:33 without looking at your card or your anchor words. If after a moment you still can't get started, then look at the anchor words or only the first word of the verse to get you going.
2. Spend a moment reflecting on the truth of this Scripture. Have you sought God's kingdom first this week? If not, what is one thing you can change to help you put God and His purposes first?
3. Pray and commit to do what God revealed to you.
4. Now recite Matthew 6:33 again like you mean it!

WEEK THREE

LONELINESS

Memory Verse

> *Neither height nor depth, nor anything else in all creation, will be able to separate us from the love of God that is in Christ Jesus our Lord.*
>
> Romans 8:39

Day One

When God Is All We Have

Read: Romans 8:35–39
Weekly memory verse: Romans 8:39

People leave. Sometimes it's by choice; sometimes it's out of their control. But they still leave. Close friends move away. Family members get sick. Relationships fall apart. These absences leave holes in our lives. Occasionally others help fill the gap. But often no one does, and loneliness rushes in.

Have you ever been lonely? Perhaps you are lonely now. Loneliness is sadness caused by the absence of companionship. That's why it can press in on us even in a crowd. The simple presence of people cannot push away loneliness. Only a caring companion can alleviate that feeling of isolation.

Even the most loving and dependable people will eventually leave us. Death and distance separate loved ones. Trouble and time tear us apart. But there is One who will never leave us or forsake us. Absolutely nothing can separate you from Jesus and His love. If you have entered into a saving relationship with Jesus, His Spirit is always present with you.

These beautiful and comforting words, penned by the Apostle Paul to the Christians in Rome, flowed from personal experience. The loving presence of Christ stayed close to him in difficult and lonely times. Paul acknowledged Christians will face hardship, loneliness, and a multitude of other trials. Yet in the midst of them, we are not alone. All others may leave us, but Jesus never will. Everyone else may be against us, but Jesus is always for us. Jesus' presence and love are sufficient.

Reflect and Apply

Are you lonely now? If so, write your thoughts about the reason for your feelings of loneliness.

Look back at today's Scripture passage. List the truths you find about God's presence and love.

With these truths in mind, list some practical ways that you can turn to God when you are feeling lonely.

Prayer Prompt

Share your feelings of loneliness with God. Ask Him to overcome your feelings with His truth and to allow you to sense His presence.

Memory Minute

Commit to memorize Romans 8:39 to internalize the truth that God will never leave you.

1. Read the verse in your favorite translation.
2. Rewrite the verse in your own words at the bottom of this page.
3. Write the verse and reference on a card for your memory system.
4. Read Romans 8:39 out loud three times.

5. Pull out the memory verse card for Matthew 6:33 from Week Two and read through it. Now recite it without looking at the card.

Day Two

Accept No Substitutes

Read: Hebrews 13:5–6
Weekly memory verse: Romans 8:39

I watched my toddler son try to pound the rectangular wooden block into the round hole of the toy workbench. He had enough coordination to hold the block over the circular opening with one hand and hit the block with the plastic hammer he held in his other hand. It was obvious to me it wouldn't fit, but he continued to try over and over. Finally, in frustration, he tossed aside the hammer and the rectangular block. He walked away without picking up the round one.

God created us for a relationship with Himself. Since He designed us to need Him, we have needs only He can satisfy. God shaped our spirits to sense His presence and communicate with Him. Therefore, we will feel lonely for the God who made us unless we are actively pursuing an intimate, growing relationship with Him.

Although made to need God, we fickle humans try to meet this need with things other than God. When distance from our Creator causes loneliness, we tend to buy something, or eat something, or start a new relationship in an attempt to fill the hole.

We buy the lie that *stuff* will meet our needs, but this falsehood only breeds loneliness. If we have some stuff, but we still feel empty, then we think we need more stuff. But only God can fully and permanently satisfy our need for Him.

When you feel lonely, don't settle for substitutes. Turn to God. He has promised to never leave you, to never forsake you. And He is faithful to keep those promises.

Reflect and Apply

Have you ever been lonely for God because you allowed distance to form in your relationship with Him? Describe this time.

What insufficient substitutes have you used in the past to try to fill God's place in your life?

Contemplate God's promises in today's Scripture passage. Beside each promise, list a situation in your life that needs God's faithful fulfillment:

- God will never leave you.
- God will never forsake you.
- God is your Helper.

Prayer Prompt

Ask God to help you recognize when you've allowed distance to creep into your relationship with Him. Ask Him to show you the things you try to use as substitutes for Him.

Memory Minute

1. Read Romans 8:39 from the card you created yesterday.
2. Identify two to four anchor words in the verse to help you remember it. Circle these words on the front of the card, and then write them on the back.

3. Recite the verse three times. The first time, read it from the card. The second time, check the anchor words on the front and then recite it. The third time, turn the card over and try to recite it by only looking at the anchor words.
4. Pull out the memory verse card for Psalm 46:1 from Week One. Try to recite it without looking at the card. Use the anchor words on the back if you need help.

Day Three

The Quality of His Presence

Read: Psalm 102:25–28
Weekly memory verse: Romans 8:39

We sat in the gallery and stared into the chamber beneath us. The Senate was in session during our visit to the Capitol. We recognized many of the people talking and milling about below, but my eyes were drawn to one face. The presence of political powerhouse Senator Edward Kennedy pushed everyone else into the background.

Elected nine times by the state of Massachusetts, Ted Kennedy served in the US Senate for almost fifty years. Committed to a life of public service, Kennedy fought tirelessly to improve education, further human rights, and provide help for disabled Americans. Whether or not we agree with his political leanings, Senator Ted Kennedy was an impressive man who earned the respect of countless Americans.

Powerful, well-known people like Ted Kennedy capture our attention. We want to watch them, hear what they have to say. Even though they are simply flawed humans like us, we even clamor to be in the presence of these people. Yet we often lack excitement about the presence of God. We take our access to the powerful Creator of the universe for granted.

The Eternal One who "laid the foundations of the earth" desires to be with you. The God who hung the sun and painted the sky with starlight knows you by name. He gently calls you to sit at His feet and share your needs, your pains, and your longings with Him. He has the power to work in your circumstances and invites you to find peace and joy in His presence. Won't you come?

Reflect and Apply

Look back through today's Scripture passage. List the characteristics and qualities of God for which the psalmist praises Him.

Considering the nature of God, what difference can His constant presence make in your life?

When feelings of loneliness begin to creep into your thoughts, what are some ways you can remind yourself of the truth that God is always with you? (For instance, you could review God's promise in Scripture that He will never leave you.)

Prayer Prompt

Ask God to overwhelm you with the "quality" and permanence of His presence.

Memory Minute

1. On the back of your Romans 8:39 memory card, draw a symbol or picture that visually represents the verse.
2. Turn the card facedown so only the anchor words you wrote yesterday and the picture you drew today can be seen. On a scratch sheet of paper, write out the verse with the reference. Refer to the anchor words and picture if you need help.

3. Now, without looking at either side of the card, recite the verse and reference from memory.
4. Try to recite Psalm 46:1 and Matthew 6:33 without looking at the cards for those verses. Use the anchor words on the back if you need help.

Day Four

Secure in His Presence

Read: Psalm 9:9–10
Weekly memory verse: Romans 8:39

When I was a girl, I took all my hurt, fear, and loneliness to my dad. If he could solve a problem, he would. If I was afraid, he would do his best to calm my fears. When I felt alone, his presence reassured me. Although Dad couldn't fix everything, he always comforted me. I felt safe and loved wrapped up in his hug. I believed nothing could harm me when Dad was near.

Your childhood experience with your father may have been vastly different from mine. In fact, you may have had a painful or nonexistent relationship with your father. Please know that this is not the way God designed it. He desires earthly fathers to reflect the loving care of our heavenly Father. Even if you lacked the attention of your earthly father, you can still experience the loving, protective presence of your heavenly Father.

Today's Scripture passage describes the Lord as a place of refuge for His people—a "stronghold in times of trouble." Picture a fortified tower on high ground, a place to which people in danger would flock. Such a fortress provides safety and security for those within because it is easily defendable against all enemies.

Those who place their trust in God are like those who take refuge from their enemies in a fortified tower. God is their safe place. Whatever dangers they face, He protects those who call on

His name. He defends us against all enemies—including loneliness. Human fathers may abandon, neglect, or fail us, but God never will. Take refuge in His loving arms.

Reflect and Apply

Describe the relationship you had with your earthly father.

Even the best earthly fathers are not perfect. In what ways does our heavenly Father surpass even the most loving earthly father?

How does the word picture of a strong fortress on high ground describe the way God loves and protects you? How could remembering this metaphor help you in times of loneliness?

Prayer Prompt

Thank God for all the ways His presence has cared for you and helped dispel loneliness in the last month.

Memory Minute

1. Recite Romans 8:39 without looking at either the front or back of your card. If you can't get started, sneak a peek at your anchor words.
2. Write the verse out on another card to put in a prominent place. Review the verse whenever you see the card.
3. Now use your unique learning style to solidify Romans 8:39 in your mind. For instance, record the verse and play it back, turn the verse into a song, or pick an object in your house to associate with the verse. I have one more idea for you—this particular verse is well-suited for hand motions!

4. Pray the verse out loud to God, adding your own thoughts and feelings as you pray.

Day Five

Intimacy in Relationship

Read: John 14:16–21
Weekly memory verse: Romans 8:39

A handful of people know things about me no one else knows. These are the friends I trust with my deepest hurts, fiercest struggles, and biggest dreams. Likewise, they trust me with the best, the saddest, and the ugliest things in their lives. This kind of transparency forges deeper trust and more intimate friendship. I am blessed to have these people in my life.

Unfortunately, none of these precious friends lives close by. Because my husband's job moves us every few years, these special women are scattered across North America. E-mail, phone, and social networking are great ways to stay in touch, but I miss our face-to-face visits over coffee. I miss not being with them.

The disciples had the physical presence of Jesus, their friend and master, for three years. He was their counselor, their advocate with the Father. When the time came for Jesus to leave them, they grew fearful. Who would guide them? Who would show them the Father? (See John 14:5–9.)

As always, God had a plan. He would not leave them alone. When Jesus left, the Holy Spirit would take His place. This Counselor would never leave. In fact, He wouldn't merely walk *among* them like Jesus did, He would be *in* them—nearer than their most intimate friend, closer than their very breath.

If you are a believer in Jesus Christ, you have this same Counselor living within you. He is your advocate with the Father, your helper, the One who gives you aid. The Spirit expresses God's love and reveals the Father to you through His permanent, abiding presence. You are never alone; God's Spirit is your constant companion.

Reflect and Apply

Think about your relationship with your closest friend. What do you share? How does she encourage you when you're together?

Contemplate the truth that God's Spirit is always with you, keeping you in constant communion with the Father. How should this truth impact your daily life?

What hurts, struggles, and dreams do you need to share with God today?

Prayer Prompt

Share your heart with God, then sit quietly and listen for Him to speak to you.

Memory Minute

1. On a scratch piece of paper, try writing Romans 8:39 without looking at your card or your anchor words. If after a moment you still can't get started, then look at the anchor words or the first word only of the verse to get you going.
2. Spend a moment reflecting on the truth of this Scripture. Think about the depth and power of God's love for you.

Allow God to embrace you with the truth that nothing and no one can come between you and His love.

3. Review your two previous verses. Recite Psalm 46:1 and Matthew 6:33 from memory. Use your anchor words only if necessary.

WEEK FOUR

ILLNESS

Memory Verse

> *I praise you because I am fearfully and wonderfully made; your works are wonderful, I know that full well.*
>
> Psalm 139:14

Day One

God's Masterpiece

Read: Psalm 139:13–16
Weekly memory verse: Psalm 139:14

Your body contains thirty-seven thousand miles of capillaries. Every second, two million blood cells die and two million more are born to take their place. Every human has a unique set of fingerprints. For you to take one step, two hundred muscles have to work. The hairs in your nose not only clean the air you breathe in, but they also warm it. The femur, the largest bone in your body, is roughly one-quarter of your height, compared to the stirrup, the smallest bone in your body, which is about the size of a grain of rice. Your heart will beat about three billion times during the course of your life.

These are just a few of the incredible facts about the human body. Even three thousand years ago, the psalmist David recognized our bodies are beautiful masterpieces of design and function. Reflecting on the miracle of birth and life moved David to acknowledge his Creator and give Him praise.

From the moment of conception to your last breath, God has ordained a purpose for your life here on this earth. And He has created your body with the ability to fulfill that purpose. He lovingly formed every part of your body, inside and out. He chose your eye color and decided how tall you would be. Your heavenly Father is intimately familiar with your body. He knows when you are healthy, and He knows when you struggle with illness or injury. You can trust Him with the body He so wonderfully made.

Reflect and Apply

What do you think is the most amazing thing about your body and how it works?

Reread Psalm 139:15–16. What does it mean to you that God made you on purpose and for a purpose?

Do you believe the One who made you is able to fulfill His purposes for you no matter your physical limitations or health? If not, in what way do you feel God is limited?

Prayer Prompt

Praise God that you are "fearfully and wonderfully made." Thank Him for the way He made your body, including its strengths and its weaknesses.

Memory Minute

For assurance that you were made just like God determined, commit to memorize Psalm 139:14.

1. Read the verse, Psalm 139:14.
2. Rewrite the verse in your own words at the bottom of this page.
3. Write the verse and reference on the same kind of card you've been using for the other memory verses.
4. Read it out loud three times.

5. Pull out your memory verse cards from the first three weeks. Read through each verse one time.

Day Two

God Is Able

Read: Mark 1:29–34
Weekly memory verse: Psalm 139:14

During my first year of college, a neurologist diagnosed me with a microscopic tumor on my pituitary gland. He told me and my parents that because of its size it was inoperable, but as long as it was there, I could never have children because I would never ovulate. Not willing to accept that outcome, my parents did two things. First, they asked the church to pray. Second, they took me to a specialist at Vanderbilt University Medical Center in Nashville. After a battery of tests, the doctor concluded, "Either you never had a tumor, or God chose to heal you." Well, the births of my three children testify to the health God gave me.

Jesus' earthly ministry shows God is willing and able to heal. Jesus cured people with everything from fever to skin disease to crippled limbs. And He healed so completely that Peter's mother-in-law was able to hop up from her sickbed and get right to work!

The body is so intricate and its systems so delicate, the fact that we wake up every morning and draw breath proves that God sustains our physical life on a daily basis. But God's care does not stop at maintenance. God still heals today. God made our bodies and He can heal them. Sometimes He works through medical science, and sometimes He cuts out the middleman and heals in a more blatantly miraculous fashion. No disease is too stubborn and no injury is too serious for our all-powerful God.

Reflect and Apply

Do you believe God has the power to heal?

Tell about a time you experienced God as a physical healer. It can be an instance from your life or the life of someone you care about.

List any illness or other physical problem you or loved ones are experiencing now. Do you believe that God cares about all these issues?

Prayer Prompt

Express to God what you believe about His power to heal. Tell Him about the physical needs on your mind today and ask Him to work.

Memory Minute

1. Read Psalm 139:14 from the card you created yesterday.
2. Spend a moment thinking about what this verse teaches about the following:
    - What you should believe about God.
    - Things you can praise or thank God for.
    - What you can pray for yourself or others.
3. Identify two to four anchor words in the verse to help you remember it. Circle these words on the front of the card, and then write them on the back.

4. Recite the verse three times. The first time, read it from the card. The second time, check the anchor words on the front and then recite it. The third time, turn the card over and try to recite it by only looking at the anchor words.
5. Time to review Psalm 46:1, your memory verse from Week One. Try to quote it from memory now. If you need help, look at your anchor words on the back of the card.

Day Three

When I Am Weak

Read: 2 Corinthians 12:7–10
Weekly memory verse: Psalm 139:14

I've been suffering with sciatica for several weeks. I'm going back and forth to the doctor, downing ibuprofen, and icing my back at regular intervals. So far, nothing has helped. It hurts to stand, but it hurts more to sit. This may be a temporary flare-up of my underlying back problem, or it could be my new normal. Do I believe God can fix this? Yes, absolutely. But I also know He may choose not to.

God worked through the Apostle Paul to heal hundreds—maybe even thousands—of people. In fact, the Bible tells us God's healing power was so strong in Paul that people were even cured when they received handkerchiefs he had touched (Acts 19:12). Yet Paul himself suffered from a chronic ailment God chose not to heal. The passage in 2 Corinthians tells us Paul repeatedly asked God to heal him, but God said no. He had a purpose. God wanted Paul to lean on Him for strength. Paul's physical weakness would not only keep him humble, but it would also point people to the power of Christ.

In any situation, God may choose to physically heal or to respond with "My grace is sufficient for you." Either way, He is seeking to work His purposes in your life. Either way, you can experience His power and love. Either way, God is still God, and He is still able.

Reflect and Apply

Have you ever doubted God because He did not act like you wanted Him to or thought He should? If you answered yes, please describe the situation.

Based on your knowledge of God through His Word, what was He able to do in the situation?

Can you think of any ways God has used this situation in your life or the lives of others to carry out His greater purposes?

Prayer Prompt

Spend time now in confession. Repent of any doubt, unbelief, or anger surrounding the situation you described in answer to the questions in the last section. Ask God to help you trust in Him and His purposes for you.

Memory Minute

1. Read Psalm 139:14 from the card you wrote on Day One.
2. On the back of the card, draw a symbol or picture that visually represents the verse.
3. Turn the card facedown so only the anchor words you wrote yesterday and the picture you drew today can be seen. On a scratch sheet of paper, write out the verse with the reference. Refer to the anchor words and picture if you need help.

4. Now, without looking at either side of the card, recite the verse and reference from memory.
5. Time to review Matthew 6:33 from Week Two. Try to quote it from memory now. If you need help, look at your anchor words on the back of the card.

Day Four

Declare His Praises

Read: Psalm 71:14–21
Weekly memory verse: Psalm 139:14

I have a dear friend with a rare form of leukemia for which there is no known cure. Right now, she is undergoing treatment in a clinical trial that consumes her thoughts and energy. Some days the medical prognosis causes her to lose hope; she allows it to rob her of her joy in Christ. But most days, she finds comfort and peace in her Savior and Lord. She clings to Him and shares with her family and friends how her God has been faithful to comfort her and renew her strength.

The psalmist endured many bitter troubles in his lifetime (Ps. 71:20). But through those trials, he experienced God in a unique way. He learned that God faithfully comforts His children and brings restoration. He felt God's power and witnessed His mighty acts. Now the psalmist had a great testimony about God to share with His children. He could not keep silent about his mighty God; he had to declare His praises!

When God allows His children to suffer trials and illness, He is not absent. God is present and working in the midst of those circumstances. Focus on God and His character instead of your illness or circumstances. Open your eyes to see His activity. Ask for His comfort and restoration. He is able to lift you up from the depths of despair. Tell your children of His marvelous deeds. Then find joy as you sing His praises!

Reflect and Apply

When you are ill or in the middle of a difficult circumstance, what is the primary thing on your mind? How do your thoughts positively or negatively affect your emotions?

How could focusing on God and His character help you as you face illness?

What would you say to others when telling them of God's marvelous deeds in your life?

Prayer Prompt

Take a few minutes to focus on God and praise Him for who He is. Meditate on His character and declare His praises!

Memory Minute

1. Recite Psalm 139:14 without looking at either the front or back of your card. If you can't get started, sneak a peek at your anchor words.
2. Write the verse out on another card. Put this verse in a prominent place where you will see it multiple times a day, such as your bathroom mirror, the refrigerator, or car dashboard. Every time you notice the card, use it as an opportunity to review the verse.
3. Time to get creative. Use your own learning style to help you memorize Psalm 139:14. If you are an auditory learner,

you could record the verse and play it back or turn the verse into a song. If you are a physical or tactile learner, pick an object in your home that represents the verse.

4. Pray the verse out loud to God, adding your own thoughts and feelings as you pray.
5. Time to review Romans 8:39 from Week Three. Try to quote it from memory now. If you need help, look at your anchor words on the back of the card.

Day Five

Spiritual Healing

Read: Isaiah 53:4–6
Weekly memory verse: Psalm 139:14

Several months ago, I was bitten by a brown recluse spider. On the first day, there was just a small, white blister. But the venom of the brown recluse can kill human tissue, and by the third day, serious infection had developed. My doctor treated the wound aggressively. On my first visit to his office, he gave me an antibiotic shot, a tetanus shot, and super-strong oral antibiotics. He also opened, drained, and packed the wound. I got the same routine the next day—minus the tetanus shot. In fact, I saw the doctor every day that week. The infection is gone, the wound is healed, but a scar remains.

The effects of illness and injury range from troublesome to life-threatening. Physical healing is a miraculous and wonderful thing, and no matter the severity, we would all rather be healthy. But, even at their worst, your health problems are temporary. However, your spiritual condition is eternal. Jesus cares greatly about your physical needs, but He is even more concerned about your spiritual needs. That's why He willingly took up your infirmities. Jesus allowed Himself to be wounded so you could be healed.

Every person has sinned (Rom. 3:23). Our sin separates us from God and brings spiritual death (Rom. 6:23). But Jesus provided for our spiritual healing by surrendering to physical death on a Roman cross two thousand years ago. His death paid our debt. Have you ever accepted the spiritual healing Jesus offers?

Reflect and Apply

What steps do you take to maintain your physical health? What about your spiritual health?

The Apostle Paul said physical training is of some value but that godliness has value for this life and eternity (1 Tim. 4:8). What are some things you can do to help make your spiritual health your top priority?

What does godliness (spiritual health) look like in the life of a believer? Do you consider yourself to be spiritually healthy?

Prayer Prompt

If you have never accepted the spiritual healing and eternal life that Jesus offers, will you do it now? In a heartfelt prayer, confess your sin, acknowledge your need for a Savior, and turn your life over to the Lordship of Jesus. If you are already a believer, ask Him to show you ways to improve your spiritual health.

Memory Minute

1. On a scratch piece of paper, try writing Psalm 139:14 without looking at your card or your anchor words. If after a moment you still can't get started, then look at the anchor words or the first word only of the verse to get you going.
2. Spend a moment reflecting on the truth of this Scripture. How does God want you to apply this verse to your life

today? Is there a truth you need to accept? Is there a decision you need to make? Is there an action you need to take? Is there an attitude you need to change?

3. Pray and commit to do what God reveals to you.
4. Now recite Psalm 139:14 again like you mean it!

WEEK FIVE

FEAR

Memory Verse

I sought the Lord, and he answered me;
he delivered me from all my fears.

Psalm 34:4

Day One

Circle of Protection

Read: Psalm 34:1–7
Weekly memory verse: Psalm 34:4

Years ago, my husband and I were camping with our two preschool daughters in the mountains of Wyoming. Sometime after midnight, noise in the camp woke me. When I whispered a question to my husband over the heads of our sleeping girls, his hushed but urgent reply quickly told me our nighttime visitor was much larger than a raccoon.

The light from the full moon cast a clear silhouette of the large black bear as she sniffed her way around the perimeter of our tent. I could see the movement of the nylon fabric and even hear her breathe as she passed close to me. Fear kept me from moving, but it also prompted prayer for protection. God heard and answered and the bear moved on.

Today we read that the angel of the Lord "encamps around those who fear him" (Ps. 34:7). When we trust God with our fears, He establishes a protective enclosure around us. The bear may have been close that night in Wyoming, but God was closer.

David, the psalmist, also knew fear. He fought wild animals to protect his sheep, hid from murderous King Saul, and stood his ground against the ferocious Philistines. Through all this, David took his fear to God. And God heard, answered, and delivered.

All of us experience fear. Sometimes the uncertainty of the future causes dread. Sometimes terrifying circumstances shake the most courageous among us. But we have a safe place to run when fears assail us. God promises to establish Himself between us and that which threatens us. Call to Him and trust in His promise.

Reflect and Apply

Describe the last time you felt fear. How was the situation resolved?

God doesn't promise we will never face frightening circumstances, but He does promise to deliver us through them. What is the difference?

What fear do you need to bring to God today? How can you actively show trust in God in the midst of this fear?

Prayer Prompt

Express your fears to God. Ask Him to help you trust Him for the outcome.

Memory Minute

Commit to memorize Psalm 34:4 to help you turn to God in times of fear.

1. Read the verse in your favorite translation.
2. Rewrite the verse in your own words at the bottom of this page.
3. Write the verse and reference on a card for your memory system.

4. Read Psalm 34:4 out loud three times.
5. Recite Psalm 46:1 from Week One. Look at your anchor words on the back of the card only if you need help.

Day Two

God Goes Before

Read: Deuteronomy 31:1–8
Weekly memory verse: Psalm 34:4

Almost every scary movie ever made has a similar scene. The hero leads the way through the dark house or dark woods or dark alley. He tells the one he is protecting to "stay behind me." Of course, the hero's intent is to keep anything bad from happening to the one he's protecting. Sometimes he is able to keep her safe, sometimes not. We have to watch the movie to see how it turns out.

Thankfully, God is much stronger than the common puny movie hero. When He goes before us, we don't have to be afraid because we know He is more than able to defeat the enemy waiting in the darkness. The Israelites' experience with God repeatedly proved His ability to deliver His people.

For forty years, He had led them through the wilderness, conquering every enemy that stood in their path. Now, as they stood poised to enter the Promised Land, God once again promised to go before them. As He had struck down the Amorites and Ammonites, God would also hand over future foes.

So with confidence in God's strength, Joshua and the Israelite army would move forward in obedience. They could fight with courage knowing that their all-powerful God led the way, knocking obstacles off the path. The way would not be easy, but God would bring them victory!

Do you have a fearful challenge or a fierce battle before you? You can take courage knowing that God will go before you. Your confidence should not be in yourself and your own ability, but in the strength of your God who leads the way.

Reflect and Apply

Is there a challenge or situation in your life that you feel inadequate to tackle? If yes, describe it.

Rewrite Deuteronomy 31:8 in your own words.

How can this truth give you courage and confidence to move forward?

Prayer Prompt

Ask God to help you find courage and confidence in His power and strength.

Memory Minute

1. Read Psalm 34:4 from the card you created yesterday.
2. Spend a moment thinking about the truths in this verse:
    - What happens when you seek the Lord?
    - What would this look like in your day-to-day life?
3. Identify two to four anchor words in the verse to help you remember the verse. Circle these words on the front of the card, and then write them on the back.

4. Recite the verse three times. The first time, read it from the card. The second time, check the anchor words on the front and then recite it. The third time, turn the card over and try to recite it by only looking at the anchor words.

Day Three

Intimate Care

Read: Psalm 91:1–10
Weekly memory verse: Psalm 34:4

Whether we think about it or not, we experience multiple forms of protection every day. Laws and law enforcement help keep criminals from harming us. Government regulations on food cut down on the number of food-borne illnesses that attack our bodies. Even our natural reflexes help us avoid accidents. But these forms of protection are general. They lack individual care and intimacy.

In contrast, God is intimately involved in the welfare of His children. Scripture describes His care as very personal. Like a mother bird draws her chicks under her wings for safety, God pulls us close to His side and gently covers us. He faithfully guards us against dangers and disease.

Because of the nature of His care, trouble fosters intimacy between us and God. In times of weakness, we learn to lean on the One who is strong. And when we lean, He gathers us in and holds us up. He encircles us with His loving arms and shields us from the enemy's arrows. Through our troubles, we develop an intimate knowledge of the God who cares for and protects us.

God does not guarantee us a life free from trouble, but He does promise to be our refuge in the midst of the storm. But we must run to Him. We must put our trust in God no matter the circumstances, knowing that nothing in our lives has slipped in without His knowledge. He has a plan for deliverance. Obediently follow His perfect will and rest in the circle of His protective shadow.

Reflect and Apply

What is the difference between God protecting us "from" trouble and God protecting us "through" trouble?

Have you experienced intimacy with God in the midst of difficult times? If so, how did your relationship with Him grow and deepen?

In what ways can you pull yourself closer to God in difficult times?

Prayer Prompt

Thank God for His gentle care and loving ways in the midst of hard times. Ask Him to teach you more about Himself when life gets difficult.

Memory Minute

1. On the back of your Psalm 34:4 memory card, draw a symbol or picture that visually represents the verse.
2. Turn the card facedown so only the anchor words you wrote yesterday and the picture you drew today can be seen. On a scratch sheet of paper, write out the verse with the reference. Refer to the anchor words and picture if you need help.
3. Now, without looking at either side of the card, recite the verse and reference from memory.

4. Today is a good day for review! Gather the cards for Psalm 46:1, Matthew 6:33, Romans 8:39, and Psalm 139:14 and carry them with you today. Try to recite each one at least three times today without looking at the cards. Use the anchor words on the back if you need help.

Day Four

Fear of Pink Scooters

Read: Matthew 10:26–31
Weekly memory verse: Psalm 34:4

One day I took Harley, our Chihuahua, for a walk. Two blocks from the house, he balked, obviously afraid, and refused to go on. Glancing ahead, I spotted the object of his fear—a small pink scooter in the middle of the sidewalk. No encouragement from me would get him moving. I ended up carrying him to "safety" on the other side of the scooter.

Harley's fear of pint-sized power toys seems completely irrational—particularly since he has no fear of our eighty-five-pound yellow lab. Boone could send him flying across the grass with one swipe of his skillet-sized paw, yet Harley acts like "king of the yard." He lunges and snaps at a powerful animal ten times his size, but he won't walk past a child's toy abandoned on the sidewalk.

Although Harley's behavior seems silly, we are prone to the same thing. Early in His ministry, Jesus tried to prepare His disciples for the persecution and trouble they would experience because of their commitment to Him. He emphasized that, compared to God, every persecutor and circumstance is powerless.

Yet still we fail to tell others about Jesus because we fear what they may think about us. We squander Christ's peace by worrying about our nation's economy. We disobey our all-powerful God, but we tremble before some temporary, earthly circumstance.

God's Word teaches us that when we stand firm in our faith in God, there's no need to fear anything. We are worth more to God than "many sparrows"; He will care for us. Therefore, let's fearlessly proclaim His name and follow Him in full obedience through every life situation.

Reflect and Apply

Think about an earthly circumstance or person you fear. How does the power of this circumstance or person to do you harm compare to the power of God to care for you?

No matter how difficult, our earthly circumstances are only temporary. How far does God's power and control reach?

Describe how keeping an eternal perspective can help us control our earthly fears.

Prayer Prompt

Ask God to help you think with an eternal scope so you can keep your earthly circumstances in perspective.

Memory Minute

1. Recite Psalm 34:4 without looking at either the front or back of your card. If you can't get started, sneak a peek at your anchor words.
2. Write the verse out on another card to put in a prominent place. Review the verse whenever you see the card.

3. Now use your unique learning style to reinforce Psalm 34:4, such as making a recording, writing a song, developing hand motions, or assigning the verse to an object in your home.
4. Find someone today who needs to hear this verse and share it with her!

Day Five

Unusual Courage

Read: Acts 4:8–13
Weekly memory verse: Psalm 34:4

I was driving on the interstate through Dallas when it happened. The pickup in front of me kicked up a five-foot strip of eighteen-wheeler tire rubber, which sent it bouncing right toward my car. With another car to my right and a concrete barrier on my left, I had nowhere to go. I did my best to keep the car steady and hit it square on. Thankfully, I was able to maintain control. I exited the interstate as quickly as possible and had my car checked out.

Sometimes we're thrust into a frightening circumstance that's unavoidable. We have no other choice but to hang on and meet it. But at other times, scary circumstances can be avoided. In some cases, avoidance is the right thing. But sometimes—like we read about in our passage today—God's will for us is to courageously take it on.

After healing a crippled man in the name of Jesus and preaching the gospel to the gathered crowd, Peter and John were arrested for telling the people about the Savior. The next morning, they were brought before the Jewish leaders for questioning. Peter and John now had a choice—they could minimize this incident by avoiding the subject of Jesus, or they could risk further trouble by courageously testifying to Christ. Peter and John chose trouble with Jesus over easy circumstances.

We learn two things from this passage that will help us take a similar stand. First, Peter was filled with the Holy Spirit. And second, their courage revealed they had been with Jesus. When we submit ourselves to the leadership of the indwelling Spirit and regularly spend time with our Lord, God will give us the courage we need to tackle the "avoidable" trouble.

Reflect and Apply

Are you facing a choice right now between avoiding a difficult circumstance and obeying God?

Think about the possible results of both your decisions. What would happen if you avoided the circumstance? What would happen if you obeyed God?

How can spending time with Jesus help you find the courage to obey God and face the avoidable trouble?

Prayer Prompt

Ask God to fill you with courage from the Holy Spirit and a desire to please Him regardless of how difficult and scary obedience will be.

Memory Minute

1. On a scratch piece of paper, try writing Psalm 34:4 without looking at your card or your anchor words. If after a moment you still can't get started, then look at the anchor words or the first word only of the verse to get you going.

2. Review your previous four memory verses. Try to recite them without looking at the cards. Use your anchor words only if necessary.
3. Choose one of these verses for personal application. At the bottom of this page or in the margin, briefly journal about how God wants to apply the truths of the verse to your life today. For instance, does it teach you something new about God? Is God asking for obedience in some specific area? Is there a sin you need to confess? Now recite the verse again!

WEEK SIX

BROKEN RELATIONSHIPS

Memory Verse

Make every effort to live in peace
with all men and to be holy;
without holiness no one will see the Lord.

Hebrews 12:14

Day One

No Relationship Is an Island

Read: Hebrews 12:14–15
Weekly memory verse: Hebrews 12:14

One of my all-time favorite movies is *Cast Away.* Tom Hanks played the role of Chuck Noland, a FedEx systems engineer. During a business trip, Chuck narrowly survives a plane crash and washes ashore on a deserted tropical island. Before he finally finds a way to make it back to civilization, Chuck spends four years completely alone, with no human interaction of any kind.

Complete isolation like this is only possible if you are the lone castaway on a deserted island. The rest of us are constantly connected to other people. Although the depths of our relationships range from superficial to intimate, no relationship exists in isolation from the others. The quality of one relationship affects all the others. For instance, an argument with one friend alters our mood and emotions, impacting our interaction with the next friend we encounter.

Today's Scripture shows us how our relationship with God directly affects all other relationships. A close, obedient relationship with God fosters holiness in our lives. When we live holy lives—lives devoted to God—we will be different from the world and its ways, and so will our relationships.

The world tells us to put ourselves first. God commands us to love each other and meet their needs. The world tells us to revenge wrongs done to us. God commands us to forgive like God has forgiven us and to get rid of all bitterness.

Are you struggling in one or more relationships? Regardless of the issue or who is at fault, the first step in improving any relationship is to check the quality of our relationship with God.

Reflect and Apply

Take a moment to evaluate your relationships. In the space below, list those in which you need God's help and direction.

Now check the quality of your relationship with God. Can you see ways that distance from God and disobedience have affected your relationships with others?

Reflect on the grace God has shown in your life. (For instance, God pursues a relationship with you, He offers undeserved forgiveness, and He promises his constant presence.) How can remembering what God has done for you help you to extend grace to others?

Prayer Prompt

Ask God to help you see the relationship issues in your life with His eyes. Ask Him to show you any sin you need to confess regarding the way you have interacted with these individuals.

Memory Minute

Commit to memorize Hebrews 12:14 to internalize the truth that the quality of your relationship with God affects all other relationships.

1. Read the verse in your favorite translation.
2. Rewrite the verse in your own words at the bottom of this page.
3. Write the verse and reference on a card for your memory system.
4. Read Hebrews 12:14 out loud three times.
5. Pull out the memory verse cards for Psalm 46:1 and Matthew 6:33. If possible, recite them without looking at the cards. Use the anchor words or the front of the card only if necessary.

Day Two

Everything You Need

Read: 2 Peter 1:3–8

Weekly memory verse: Hebrews 12:14

I read the top of the box: "Includes absolutely everything you need to host a fun and exciting murder mystery party!" Really? Everything? The box did indeed include invitations, instructions, character booklets, recipes, and evidence to help find the killer. It was a good start, but of course it did not include the actual guests or the food to make the recipes. I provided my own friends and food, and the evening was a success!

In his letter, Peter wrote that God provides Christians with everything—and he really means everything—we need to live a godly life that pleases Him. God's power working in us shapes our character to be like His. So instead of acting like the world, we can act like Jesus. We can treat others like Jesus treated others. Our relationships can be strong and loving.

We also learn from today's passage that God expects us to cooperate with His working in our lives. He has given us the Holy Spirit to purify us and mold our character, but He calls us to cooperate with His activity. Peter told his readers to "make every effort" to add godly characteristics to their faith.

God gives us what we need to be kind and act loving toward others, but we must follow His direction as He leads us in our relationships. For instance, the Holy Spirit gives us the self-control not to respond to our spouses with angry words, but we must hold our tongues. As we obey God and let Him have more and more control over our relationships, they will strengthen and deepen. That's exactly what we need!

Reflect and Apply

Do you ever feel like loving, godly relationships are out of your reach? What does God's Word say about it?

The Holy Spirit promises to provide you with everything you need to be kind and loving in your relationships. If provision is the Holy Spirit's responsibility, what is yours?

Have you ever stubbornly done the opposite from what you felt God leading you to do in a relationship? What was the outcome?

Prayer Prompt

Thank God for His provision in your life. Ask His forgiveness for the times you've ignored His direction in your relationships.

Memory Minute

1. Read Hebrews 12:14 from the card you created yesterday.
2. Identify two to four anchor words in the verse to help you remember it. Circle these words on the front of the card and then write them on the back.
3. Recite the verse three times. The first time, read it from the card. The second time, check the anchor words on the front and then recite it. The third time, turn the card over and try to recite it by only looking at the anchor words.

4. Pull out the cards for Romans 8:39 and Psalm 139:14 from Week Three and Week Four. Try to recite them without looking at the cards. Use the anchor words on the back if you need help.

Day Three

Leave the Rest to God

Read: Romans 12:17–21
Weekly memory verse: Hebrews 12:14

The idiom "it takes two to tango" describes the nature of relationships. The individuals must be "dancing" together to avoid stepping on each other's toes. Both must work to keep in step, and both must correct missteps when things go awry.

Whether it's a marriage, friendship, or business partnership, any relationship requires at least two individuals. By definition, "relationship" refers to an association, involvement, or emotional connection between people. Therefore, when problems arise in a relationship, both people must work to correct them.

Sometimes though, one member may not be willing to do her part to heal the relationship. He may refuse to acknowledge his part in the problems. She may have little desire to continue the relationship. Or he may continue to treat you badly. But God's command to us through Paul is clear: "As far as it depends on you, live at peace with everyone."

Paul's words acknowledge that both people in a relationship should do their part. But he also tells us to act Christlike no matter how the other person behaves. God will hold us responsible for our actions. Even if others do us evil, God calls us to treat them with love and kindness. Revenge and retribution are solely God's territory.

If problems come to a relationship, do everything you can to resolve the issue and restore peace in a godly way. Trust God to work powerfully in both of your lives. Follow His guidance. Then if the other person still refuses full reconciliation, leave the rest to God. In His time, God will bring complete justice.

Reflect and Apply

Are you currently in a troubled relationship in which you feel you are the only one working to resolve the problems?

How does today's Scripture passage encourage you to continue at this task?

Look back through today's Scripture. In this particular relationship, are you acting in any way that infringes on God's area of responsibility?

Prayer Prompt

Ask the Father to help you show love and kindness to someone who does not always act that way toward you.

Memory Minute

1. On the back of your Hebrews 12:14 memory card, draw a symbol or picture that visually represents the verse.
2. Turn the card facedown so only the anchor words you wrote yesterday and the picture you drew today can be seen. On a scratch sheet of paper, write out the verse with the reference. Refer to the anchor words and picture if you need help.

3. Now, without looking at either side of the card, recite the verse and reference from memory.
4. Try to recite Psalm 34:4 from Week Five without looking at the card. Use the anchor words on the back if you need help.

Day Four

Love Is . . .

Read: 1 Corinthians 13:4–7
Weekly memory verse: Hebrews 12:14

Do you remember the old "Love Is" cartoons? The drawings, which always featured the same little boy and girl characters, included a one-sentence caption that described love. For instance, a poster that hung in my bedroom during my teen years read: "Love is . . . never having to say you're sorry."

The famous cartoons' descriptions for love were varied and imaginative. *Love is . . . when his world revolves around yours. Love is . . . enjoying the simple things in life together. Love is . . . giving him another chance.* These sentiments may make cute posters, but their definitions for love are far from biblical.

The Greek word translated as "love" in 1 Corinthians 13 is *agape*, the same word used to describe God's love for us. Agape is love expressed in deliberate action. Agape seeks the welfare of others. Agape does not depend on emotion or the other person's character, but instead it is love of volition. Agape is not a feeling but a choice.

In our relationships, sometimes we *feel* loving toward the other person and sometimes we don't. Sometimes the other person's behavior pushes us past our limits for patience and kindness. In fact, sometimes his or her behavior would make the strongest Christian angry enough to walk away. But according to God's

Word, no matter how we *feel* toward him or her, we should always *act* loving.

We do not deserve God's love, but He has chosen to love us. *But God demonstrates his own love for us in this: While we were still sinners, Christ died for us* (Rom. 5:8). This is agape, the pattern of love God calls us to follow.

Reflect and Apply

Make a list of the words and phrases in today's passage used to describe agape love.

How different would your love for others look if you based it on God's pattern of love?

What kind of changes could it foster in your relationships?

Prayer Prompt

Ask God to overwhelm you today with His love for you. Then ask Him to help you show that love to someone else.

Memory Minute

1. Recite Hebrews 12:14 without looking at either the front or back of your card. If you can't get started, sneak a peek at your anchor words.
2. Write the verse out on another card to place in a prominent place. Review the verse whenever you see the card.
3. Now use your unique learning style to reinforce Hebrews 12:14, such as making a recording, writing a song,

developing hand motions, or assigning the verse to an object in your home.

4. Act on the truth in this week's memory verse. Ask God to show you something you can do to foster peace with someone in your life. Commit to do it before the week is up.

Day Five

Love Is Action

Read: 1 John 3:14–18
Weekly memory verse: Hebrews 12:14

Years ago, country singer Clint Black wrote and recorded a song titled "Something That We Do." One verse from the song says:

> I remember well the day we wed
> I can see that picture in my head
> Love isn't just those words we said
> It's something that we do

Whether he intended it or not, his lyrics reflect a biblical principle of the nature of love. Anyone can say those three little words, but real love is shown by what we do.

Today's Scripture reading teaches us that real love willingly gives for another's benefit. Jesus Christ's sacrificial death is the ultimate expression of love. He willingly gave His life so we might live.

Jesus' act of love is also our example. We learn how to love from His love. God calls us to give sacrificially as Jesus gave to us. God probably won't ask us to literally give our lives for someone else, but He does regularly call us to let go of what we have to meet the needs of others.

Will you give of your time to someone who needs a listening ear? Will you give your resources to someone who is hungry or can't pay the doctor's bill? Will you open your home or your heart or your wallet to help someone today?

Jesus' act of love prepared the way for our relationship with God. Love in action is also the basis of real relationships in our own lives. When we love others like Jesus loved us, our relationships will flourish.

Reflect and Apply

Write a biblical definition of love in your own words.

Evaluate the way you love the people in your life. Do you love them with deeds and not just words?

Now think of that struggling relationship. How can you show love to that person today?

Prayer Prompt

Ask God for the opportunity to show love to someone who needs it today.

Memory Minute

We have come to the halfway point in our time together. You have hidden six verses from God's Word in your heart! Let's reinforce them today. By the time you go to sleep tonight, review each verse twice.

WEEK SEVEN

UNCERTAINTY

Memory Verse

Now to him who is able to do immeasurably more than all we ask or imagine, according to his power that is at work within us, to him be glory in the church and in Christ Jesus throughout all generations, for ever and ever! Amen.

Ephesians 3:20–21

Day One

The Sure Thing

Read: Ephesians 3:16–21
Weekly memory verse: Ephesians 3:20–21

Consumers love the promise of a "money-back guarantee." We want assurance we will receive the quality, content, or benefit promised by a product or service. If the outcome turns out to be less than we expected, then we have something to fall back on. Sadly, sometimes even a "money-back guarantee" isn't even a sure thing.

Life is full of uncertainty—much of it more serious than whether or not our breakfast cereal will help us drop five pounds in two weeks. Computers crash. Big companies go bankrupt. Health fanatics get sick. Tsunamis wipe out entire countries.

Nothing in this physical life is completely dependable. Our earthly circumstances may be uncertain, but our spiritual circumstances are sure. The physical is temporary and transient, but the spiritual is certain and eternal.

In today's passage, Paul reminds us of the certainty of God's power and presence in our uncertain lives. From His abundant riches, God strengthens us with His power to meet uncertainty head-on. Through every unpredictable circumstance of life, Jesus' loving presence sustains us.

No matter how uncertain our earthly future may loom, God's love is certainly bigger. No matter how much devastation our current situation may hold, God is able to work in greater ways than we can even imagine. In the midst of uncertain times, stand on the certainty of God's power and loving presence. "Now to him who is able!"

Reflect and Apply

Make a list of any "uncertain" circumstances in your life.

According to today's passage, how can God provide you with certainty in uncertain times?

Contemplate the width, length, height, and depth of God's love for you. How does His love encourage you in uncertain times?

Prayer Prompt

Talk with God about one specific "uncertainty" in your life. Ask Him to do "immeasurably more" than you can ask or imagine.

Memory Minute

Commit to memorize Ephesians 3:20–21 to remind you of God's power available to you.

1. Read the verses in your favorite translation.
2. Rewrite the verses in your own words at the bottom of this page.
3. Write the verse and reference on a card for your memory system.
4. Read Ephesians 3:20–21 out loud three times.

5. Recite Psalm 46:1 from Week One and Matthew 6:33 from Week Two. Look at your anchor words on the back of the cards only if you need help.

Day Two

Our Forever King

Read: Psalm146:3–10
Weekly memory verse: Ephesians 3:20–21

He led his first army into battle at a mere sixteen years of age. Two years later, his father gave him his first command post as a general. At the age of twenty, Alexander ascended to the Macedonian throne. For the next thirteen years, he used his military prowess to create one of the largest empires in ancient history.

Never defeated in battle, Alexander the Great was undeniably one of the greatest military leaders of all time. But we will never know how far his military skill would have taken him. In 323 BC, at the age of thirty-three, Alexander succumbed to a raging fever. The exact circumstances of his death are debated. Some historians say he died of natural causes. Others hint at conspiracy and poison.

During his life, Alexander the Great appeared to be unstoppable. He defeated every army he faced. He conquered every city he attacked. But even Alexander's future was uncertain. Like every other human that has ever lived, Alexander the Great had his limits.

But we have a King without limits. He can be completely trusted because He is all-powerful and utterly faithful. This trustworthy King, the maker of heaven and earth, is worthy of our trust. From generation to generation, the Lord cares for the needy and sustains the weak. His righteous reign will never end.

Your current circumstances may be shaky. The days ahead may be insecure. But you can place your uncertain future in His certain hands. Because the Lord reigns forever!

Reflect and Apply

Is there something or someone you depended on that has recently let you down?

List all the righteous acts of our Forever King that you can find in today's passage.

Which of these faithful acts of God do you most need today? Why?

Prayer Prompt

Like the psalmist in today's passage, spend a few minutes praising our Forever King!

Memory Minute

1. Read Ephesians 3:20–21 from the card you created yesterday.
2. Spend a moment thinking about the truths in this verse:
    - How much is God able to do in your life?
    - How should you respond to this truth?

3. Identify two to four anchor words in the verse to help you remember the verse. Circle these words on the front of the card and then write them on the back.
4. Recite the verse three times. The first time, read it from the card. The second time, check the anchor words on the front and then recite it. The third time, turn the card over and try to recite it by only looking at the anchor words.

Day Three

Best-Laid Plans

Read: Proverbs 16:3, 9
Weekly memory verse: Ephesians 3:20–21

Several years ago, we decided to take a cruise to celebrate our daughter's graduation from high school. The entire family would spend seven days in the Caribbean on a floating resort! This trip took months of careful planning. We researched the cruise and excursions. We carefully picked the flight that would get us to the departure city on time. We checked the weather to pack the right clothing.

Finally, the time arrived. We loaded the luggage and went to the airport. But one problem after another arose. We suffered through mechanical trouble, overbooking, and weather issues. After hours of trying everything, our disappointed family put the luggage back in the car and went home. All our careful planning could not get us on that ship because so many things were simply out of our control.

King Solomon learned this, too. Even though we like to plan, our control is limited. In fact, you may be frustrated or anxious right now because you feel you have no control over your life. Be encouraged and take comfort in this firm truth: our God has complete control.

Today's Scripture passage shows us how God's people can trust Him with the plans we make. First, we should seek God's direction as we plan. The word "commit" in 16:3 implies a humble dependence on God for the direction of our lives. Ask for His will and follow it. God blesses the plans that please Him. Second, leave the outcome up to God. Our plans still may change, but we can trust that God is in control.

Reflect and Apply

Have you ever made plans that fell apart? How did that make you feel?

Take a moment to reflect on the outcome. In what ways can you see God's hand in it?

Do you regularly seek God's direction in your plans? In what ways do you do that?

Prayer Prompt

Talk to God now about plans you've been considering. Humbly ask His will for these plans.

Memory Minute

1. One good way to tackle longer verses is to break the passage into smaller chunks. Ephesians 3:20–21 can be broken down into four phrases. On a scratch piece of paper, write each phrase on a separate line.
2. Spend a few moments working on one phrase at a time.
3. Without looking at the phrases or your memory card, try to recite the entire verse and reference from memory.

4. Recite Romans 8:39 from Week Three and Psalm 139:14 from Week Four. Look at your anchor words on the back of the card only if you need help.

Day Four

Green in Drought

Read: Jeremiah 17:7–8
Weekly memory verse: Ephesians 3:20–21

For the last several years, Texas and other parts of the southwest United States have experienced extreme drought conditions. The results have been devastating. Cattle died in the fields. Wildfires destroyed homes and businesses. Drinking water supplies reached dangerously low levels. Crops withered away. Birds even changed their migration patterns.

Unfortunately, as scientists predict the drought conditions will continue, worry rises over our water supply, the cost of food, and wildlife survival. The government seeks ways to conserve water. Individuals prepare to deal with the ongoing effects of drought, such as brown lawns and dirty cars. Avid gardeners seek drought-resistant plants and watch their trees for signs of stress.

Trees with deep and penetrating roots have a much greater chance of surviving drought than others. This kind of root system absorbs water more effectively and loses less water to the soil. Lack of rain does not affect these drought-resistant trees like it affects those with shallow root systems.

Today's Scripture shows us how we can be "drought-resistant" people of God. We may not know when rain will fall or when the economy will improve or when peace will come to the Middle

East, but we don't have to fear this uncertainty. God is certain of both the outcome and the timing.

In the midst of drought, entrench yourself firmly in God. Trust Him to provide faithfully for your needs. He will lovingly sustain you. You don't have to worry or fear when difficulties come and the future looks bleak. God promises to care for those who put their confidence in Him.

Reflect and Apply

Look back at today's Scripture passage. List the blessings God promises for those who put their trust and confidence in God.

What are some ways you can send your "roots" deep into God during times of uncertainty?

Consider the testimony your life will be to others as you continue to "produce fruit" in the midst of drought. Who in your life would benefit from this example of God's faithfulness?

Prayer Prompt

Ask God to help you remain confident in Him even when you are surrounded by "drought" conditions.

Memory Minute

1. Recite Ephesians 3:20–21 without looking at either the front or back of your card. If you can't get started, sneak a peek at your anchor words.
2. Write the verse out on another card to place in a prominent location. Review the verse whenever you see the card.

3. Now use your unique learning style to reinforce Ephesians 3:20–21, such as making a recording, writing a song, developing hand motions, or assigning the verse to an object in your home.
4. Find someone today who is experiencing drought conditions in her life. Share Ephesians 3:20 with her!

Day Five

God's Perfect Planning

Read: Acts 17:24–28
Weekly memory verse: Ephesians 3:20–21

In almost thirty years of marriage, my husband and I have moved seven times. We began our marriage in southern Louisiana, the heart of Cajun Country. Then my husband's job took us on a crazy course across North America and back again. Sometimes we felt ready to move. Other times we wanted to stay put.

Many tears, extreme emotions, and difficult challenges accompanied each move, but hindsight provides great perspective. Looking back, we can see God's hand in each change. We learned He used the job to put our family where He wanted us. Our experience with God taught us He can be trusted to do what's best for us. As we trusted Him more, our attitudes toward the moves changed, too. Even though the change itself was difficult, we grew to want His will for our family.

During more than one move, God used the truths from today's passage to sustain me. If God can raise and topple nations to carry out His purposes, He can certainly orchestrate my life as He sees fit. If God is able to determine the exact point in history for a king to come to power and the geographical boundaries for His empire, God is able to choose a city for our family and the time for us to live there.

Paul wanted the polytheistic Athenians to recognize the Creator's active determination in history and His desire for mankind to know Him. The one, true God needed nothing from them, but they needed Him for everything. Things haven't changed. God still works in history. He still orchestrates your life and meets your needs so you will "seek him and perhaps reach out for him and find him."

Reflect and Apply

Look back through today's passage. List the ways God is involved in human history.

Think back over the course of your life. List some ways you can see God's activity in your past.

How did God's involvement in your life help you know Him better?

Prayer Prompt

Thank God that He has a plan for your life. Ask Him to help you see His intimate involvement.

Memory Minute

1. On a scratch piece of paper, try writing Ephesians 3:20–21 without looking at your card or your anchor words. If after a moment you still can't get started, then look at the anchor words or only the first word of the verse to get you going.

2. Recite Psalm 34:4 from Week Five and Hebrews 12:14 from Week Six. Look at your anchor words on the back of the card only if you need help.
3. Flip through all seven of your memory verse cards. Pick out the one card you have struggled the most to memorize. Recite it three times.

WEEK EIGHT

WEARINESS

Memory Verse

Come to me, all you who are weary and burdened, and I will give you rest.

Matthew 11:28

Day One

Are You Weary?

Read: Matthew 11:28–30
Weekly memory verse: Matthew 11:28

We recently welcomed our first grandchild into the world. He is a good baby and our daughter is doing a great job, but like all new moms, she longs for a solid night's sleep. The lack of sufficient, uninterrupted sleep clouds her days with physical weariness.

I know many others experiencing their own forms of weariness. For instance, my friend Julie continues her fight with a terminal illness. A mother and father in our church struggle with their teenager's ongoing rebellious behavior. A man I know patiently and lovingly cares for his wife with Alzheimer's disease. A sweet young couple I met recently waits for a child of their own.

Jesus knows that weariness is a common human condition. It can be caused by a heavy struggle, a toilsome labor, or an overwhelming burden. Exhaustion, grief, or trouble accompanies this kind of bone-deep weariness. And it can be physical, emotional, or spiritual.

Are you weary? Do you feel weighed down by a burden you're struggling to carry by yourself? Come to Jesus and find rest. Jesus offers us rest for this life and the life to come. He gives relief from our earthly labor and freedom for our souls.

To receive Jesus' rest, to ease our weariness, we need to take on His yoke of discipleship. When we follow Him in obedience,

He takes our weary load. He bears our grief and pain. Aren't you tired? Don't wait any longer. Trade your heavy burden for the light, gentle yoke of Christ.

Reflect and Apply

Are there any ongoing sources of weariness in your life right now? If so, name it below. If not, list the name of a friend or family member who needs relief from his or her burden.

Describe how this weariness affects you (or your friend).

Picture Jesus taking your load. Hand Him your grief, pain, and overall weariness. Now pick up His yoke of discipleship; commit to obedience.

Prayer Prompt

Thank Jesus for His invitation of rest. Ask Him to show you how to give Him your burden and take His yoke.

Memory Minute

Commit to memorize Matthew 11:28 as a constant reminder of Jesus' invitation to rest.

1. Read Matthew 11:28 in your favorite translation.
2. Rewrite the verse in your own words at the bottom of this page.
3. Write the verse and reference on a card for your memory system.
4. Read Matthew 11:28 out loud three times.

5. Identify two to four anchor words in the verse to help you remember it. Circle these words on the front of the card and then write them on the back.

Day Two

Strength of Your Heart

Read: Psalm 73:12–26
Weekly memory verse: Matthew 11:28

Do you ever simply get weary of life? Work, family problems, busy days, and health issues keep piling up until sometimes you just want to crawl back under the covers and stay in bed. Or maybe, like the psalmist, you are fed up with the evil and injustice of the world around you. You've had it, but you don't know what to do with it.

The prosperity and arrogance of the evil people around the psalmist wearied him (see verses 1–16). Their seemingly carefree life plagued and confused him. He carefully worked to stay pure before God, but what had it gotten him? With a bitter heart, the psalmist took his questions and disappointments of life to God.

When the psalmist entered God's sanctuary for prayer and worship (73:17), his entire perspective changed. His temporary troubles seemed small compared to eternity. The pain and intensity of his present circumstances dimmed in the light of God's presence.

God wants us to take our questions, disappointments, and frustrations to Him. The process of grappling over our weary circumstances with God grows us spiritually and draws us closer to Him. The deeper intimacy we forge produces comfort and fresh strength to keep going. Our circumstances may not change, but God prepares us to meet them.

Although God can change your circumstances, He does not make that promise. God does promise to bless and strengthen you with His presence. God Himself is your "portion," your great reward. Even if your physical circumstances continue to deteriorate, you have more than you need. God Himself is your reward. Come into His presence. Bring your pain. Allow Him to strengthen your heart.

Reflect and Apply

How can considering your present circumstances in light of eternity change your perspective?

When was the last time you simply sat still with God and basked in His presence?

List ways you can be strengthened through a more intimate relationship with God.

Prayer Prompt

Ask God to help you see your current circumstances with an eternal perspective.

Memory Minute

1. Read Matthew 11:28 from the card you wrote it on yesterday.
2. Spend a moment thinking about the truths in this verse:

    a. What does Jesus invite you to do?

b. What keeps you from bringing your burdens to Him?

3. Now, without looking at either side of the card, recite the verse and reference from memory.
4. Share the verse by text or e-mail with someone today who needs this particular encouragement from God's Word.

Day Three

Restores Your Soul

Read: Psalm 23:1–4
Weekly memory verse: Matthew 11:28

Our family loves dogs. Between us and our grown children, we have six canines. Family gatherings can get a bit crazy. Remi will eat any dog food he can get his snout in. Sadie, the smallest, pesters all the other dogs. Harley is a loner and usually wanders off by himself. To keep things running smoothly, we must consider the needs, quirks, and personalities of each dog. The "flock" requires constant attention.

The ancient shepherd worked diligently to meet the individual needs of his sheep. He knew the weaker ones and the ones that would lag behind. He made sure each sheep had plenty of food and water. In Bible times, the shepherd also regularly risked his life to protect his sheep from dangers like lions, hyenas, and desert terrain.

The shepherd also had a unique bond with his flock. Since he often spent long periods of time in isolation with his sheep, they developed a close relationship. The shepherd knew each sheep by name, and the sheep could distinguish their shepherd's voice from the voices of other shepherds. The shepherd provided, protected, guided, and disciplined.

The psalmist David paints a beautiful image of the shepherd to show how God cares for us, His sheep. God's presence in our lives is extremely personal. He knows our unique needs and how to meet them. When danger lurks, He protects us. When we're tired, the Shepherd leads us to rest. When we grow weary from wandering, He "restores" our souls by drawing us back to His side.

Reflect and Apply

Look back through today's passage and list all the ways the Good Shepherd cares for you.

Which of the things on the list do you need today?

Is your soul weary from wandering away from God? Consider the amount of time you spend with the Shepherd and the quality of your "followship."

Prayer Prompt

Confess any sins and areas of disobedience to God now. Ask Him to forgive your wanderings and restore your weary soul.

Memory Minute

Time for review! Pull out all eight memory cards. Beginning with Psalm 46:1 from Week One, try to recite each verse without looking at the card. If you have trouble, use your anchor words and picture on the back. Only look at the verse if necessary.

Day Four

Help in Weakness

Read: Romans 8:26–28
Weekly memory verse: Matthew 11:28

According to the weather forecast, a big storm would be coming through that afternoon. Worried that the small fruit dotting the branches of my newly potted lemon and lime trees might not survive the wind and potential hail, I decided to move them under the roofline close to the house. Just one problem—I was too weak to move the pots by myself. Thankfully, my husband was home and gladly offered to help. Lifting together, we easily moved the trees to safety.

Our physical strength is limited. In fact, human limitations make us weak and vulnerable in many areas. Our physical limitations can wreak havoc with our joints and muscles, causing injury and pain. Our mental limitations prevent us from solving complex problems, such as finding a cure for the common cold. Our spiritual limitations keep us from knowing how to pray at times when we desperately need God. But God has provided an Intercessor to come alongside us in our spiritual weakness.

Sometimes when problems overwhelm us, our prayers feel limited. We struggle to comprehend the real need. We aren't sure what God's will is in the situation. We desperately need something, but we don't even know how to ask God for help. Our weary souls groan, but words won't come. Our Intercessor, the

Holy Spirit, intercedes with God on our behalf. He understands the problem inside and out. We may not know how to pray in accordance with the Father's will, but our Intercessor's prayers align perfectly.

Even when you don't know what to pray, come to God in prayer. Allow your Intercessor to come alongside you and do His work. Then, in your weakness, God will demonstrate His strength.

Reflect and Apply

When was the last time you struggled in prayer for a specific need?

What is God's promise to us in today's Scripture passage?

How can you cooperate with the Holy Spirit in prayer?

Prayer Prompt

Ask the Father to help you recognize the presence and activity of the Holy Spirit when you pray. Thank God for His help in your weakness.

Memory Minute

1. On the back of your Matthew 11:28 memory card, draw a symbol or picture that visually represents the verse.
2. Turn the card facedown so only the anchor words you wrote earlier and the picture you drew today can be seen. On a scratch sheet of paper, write out the verse with the reference. Refer to the anchor words and picture if you need help.
3. Now, without looking at either side of the card, recite the verse and reference from memory.

Day Five

Not Grow Weary

Read: Isaiah 40:27–31
Weekly Memory Verse: Matthew 11:28

About fifteen years ago, a few friends talked me into signing up for a 10K race. We ran together several times a week to "train" for the big day. All four of us ran and finished. We were so happy with ourselves that we decided a half-marathon should be our next challenge. About a month later, I injured my foot. That was the end of my running career.

One of the women in our little group eventually ran a marathon and did great. I cheered for her from afar and was genuinely excited about her accomplishment. She has much more strength and lung capacity than I do. But she could not run indefinitely. At some point, she would tire. Her body would grow weary, and she would have to stop running.

We puny humans know all about "tired" and "weary." No matter our age, ability, or strength, every single one of us has a limit, a point where we can go no further. But our God never grows weary. His strength has no limits, and His understanding knows no bounds.

"Do you not know? Have you not heard?" The Creator who formed the heavens sees our earthly struggles. The eternal King, who knows the beginning of time from the end, cares when we grow tired and weary. The God of Jacob picks us up when we stumble and fall. The all-powerful Lord shares His unlimited strength with you, His child. Put your hope in Him and renew your strength from His infinite supply.

Reflect and Apply

What life situations seem to drain your strength more quickly than others?

Do you go to God for help first, or do you tend to seek it from other places?

What is God's promise in these verses? Will you commit to look to Him first for strength?

Prayer Prompt

Use the truths in today's passage to praise God for who He is. For instance, praise God that He alone is the Creator.

Memory Minute

1. Use your unique learning style to reinforce Matthew 11:28, such as making a recording, writing a song, developing hand motions, or assigning the verse to an object in your home.
2. Now recite Matthew 11:28 three times without looking at your card.

WEEK NINE

WORRY

Memory Verse

Cast all your anxiety on him
because he cares for you.

1 Peter 5:7

Day One

Humble Submission

Read: 1 Peter 5:5–7
Weekly memory verse: 1 Peter 5:7

My own pride has caused me much pain over the years. Sometimes the pain comes quickly and is relatively minor. As soon as I acknowledge my prideful folly, I can put the incident behind me. For instance, once I refused a man's offer to lift my heavy suitcase. When I attempted to "prove my strength," I pulled a muscle. My pride quickly dissolved.

Other times, my pride prolongs the pain and kicks off a season of unnecessary worry and anxiety. Scripture clearly tells us to lean on God and trust Him during every circumstance of our lives. Yet, over and over I've tried to prove myself strong and self-sufficient by handling things my own way. My pride only multiplied my worries.

Anytime we stubbornly cling to our own "wisdom," we are rejecting God's leadership. When we demand that God work on our timetable in a given situation, we boldly declare that we know better than the Creator of the universe. We foolishly trade God's powerful plans for our weak attempts. We exchange God's perfect peace for anxiety.

You can lay your worries at God's feet when you obediently submit to His leadership and trust Him to lovingly work in your life. God is not indifferent to your suffering. He cares about every difficult situation and painful circumstance. Refuse to allow pride to block God's activity in your life. Prayerfully, throw your worry and your will at His feet. Choose humble trust over prideful self-sufficiency. Cling to the truth that God cares for you and will graciously work in His time and way.

Reflect and Apply

Has your pride caused you unnecessary pain and worry in the past? If so, what happened?

Make a list of every situation that is currently causing you worry or anxiety.

Who is more capable of working in this situation, you or God? Will you trust Him to powerfully and lovingly work for your good?

Prayer Prompt

Ask God to help you cast your worry and your pride at His feet today.

Memory Minute

Commit to memorize 1 Peter 5:7 to internalize the wonderful truth that God cares about every aspect of your life.

1. Read the verse in your favorite translation.
2. Rewrite the verse in your own words at the bottom of this page.
3. Write the verse and reference on a card for your memory system.
4. Read 1 Peter 5:7 out loud three times.

Day Two

Joy Overcomes Worry

Read: Psalm 94:16–19
Weekly memory verse: 1 Peter 5:7

Several months ago, two men tried to break into our house in the middle of the afternoon. I was home and interrupted their efforts when I encountered their lookout in the front yard. For a while after, I struggled with anxiety over what could have happened if they had gotten inside. I even began to worry about possible future attempts.

Evil plagues the world. Everything from celebrity scandal and political corruption to oppressive regimes and terrorist plots fill the news. Men and women, consumed with the desire for power and money, will do whatever it takes to possess them. Their arsenal of weapons includes lying, stealing, cheating, and even killing. Spending even just a small amount of time watching television or reading the headlines can leave us overwhelmed with anxiety. "Will evil win?" "When will wickedness knock on my door?"

In today's passage, the psalmist expresses similar feelings. Wicked people sought to harm him. Arrogant evildoers crushed those around him. "Who would stop them?" Then the psalmist remembered his Helper. When he felt like he was slipping over the edge, the Lord caught him. God's unfailing love supported him and eased his anxiety. God's comfort replaced his worry with joy.

If we dwell on the apparent victory of evil, worry will overwhelm us. If we focus on the evildoer rather than the Almighty God, anxiety will smother us. Our God, who has all authority and power, is our advocate. Turn to Him when worry surfaces. Reach for Him when anxiety creeps in. His love will support you. His comfort will bring joy to your soul.

Reflect and Apply

Have you ever personally been affected by the actions of evil people? If so, did you struggle afterward with anxiety?

What situations in your community or across the world cause you anxiety now?

List truths about God's power and authority you can cling to when worry plagues you.

Prayer Prompt

Confess any worry and anxiety to God now. Ask Him to comfort you and replace your worry with His joy.

Memory Minute

1. Read 1 Peter 5:7 from the card you created yesterday.
2. Identify two to four anchor words in the verse to help you remember it. Circle these words on the front of the card and then write them on the back.
3. Recite the verse three times. The first time, read it from the card. The second time, check the anchor words on the front

and then recite it. The third time, turn the card over and try to recite it by only looking at the anchor words.

Day Three

Peace of the Rock

Read: Isaiah 26:1–4
Weekly memory verse: 1 Peter 5:7

Perched on a hillside, our neighborhood in Canada looked out over the Bow River Valley and across to the glorious Rocky Mountains. The view was breathtaking, panoramic, and peaceful. Many people longed to escape the city living of Calgary and move out to our small town. Every year, new developments popped up all around the hills and bluffs on the outskirts of Cochrane to meet the demand.

Unfortunately, some people did not gain the peace they moved to find. One developer failed to do his homework. Unstable ground on one particular hillside caused cracks in foundations and driveways. Several homes sustained even more damage when they slid slightly downhill. Both the developer and the homeowners suffered financial loss. Many other residents lost sleep worrying whether the ground beneath their homes was firm or shaky.

Believers who have built their lives on the eternal Rock can sleep soundly at night. When we plant our trust firmly in our faithful God, we will not be disappointed. His promise to "keep in perfect peace" those who trust in Him is a commitment to guard, preserve, and hold us close. God keeps watch to protect His children from danger. He stands guard to defend us from our enemies.

Do you worry about potential threats or unstable circumstances? Draw close to God. Allow Him to wash away your worry and fill you with a sense of well-being and security. Plant your feet on the Solid Foundation and place your confidence in His faithfulness. Our God will not be moved.

Reflect and Apply

What unstable circumstances in your life have potential to wreak havoc and steal your peace?

List truths about God's stability and faithfulness.

How can reflecting on these truths ease your worry and restore peace?

Prayer Prompt

Ask God to help you peacefully rest in His faithfulness.

Memory Minute

1. On the back of your 1 Peter 5:7 memory card, draw a symbol or picture that visually represents the verse.
2. Turn the card facedown so only the anchor words you wrote yesterday and the picture you drew today can be seen. On a scratch sheet of paper, write out the verse with the reference. Refer to the anchor words and picture if you need help.
3. Now, without looking at either side of the card, recite the verse and reference from memory.

4. Try to recite Psalm 46:1, Matthew 6:33, and Romans 8:39 from the first three weeks without looking at the cards. Use the anchor words on the back if you need help.

Day Four

Prayer Changes Everything

Read: Philippians 4:4–7
Weekly memory verse: 1 Peter 5:7

Our Savior experienced betrayal, temptation, and rejection. He endured pain, hunger, and loss. Jesus understands the difficult circumstances we face because He faced them, too. And He took it all to His Father in prayer. Jesus rejected the worry and anxiety His circumstances could easily produce by spending time in God's presence. We can't always choose our circumstances, but we can choose whether or not to allow those circumstances to fill us with anxiety.

According to the apostle Paul, prayer is the answer to anxiety and worry. "Don't be anxious . . . pray instead." He wasn't talking about perfunctory prayer. Routine, superficial prayer accomplishes nothing. But when we come to God with humble gratitude and an attitude of worship, we enter His presence. There, in His presence, we find His peace. Peace that the world cannot understand. Peace that seems impossible in the midst of overwhelming circumstances. Yet God graciously gives it to us, His children.

Are you worried about one of your children? Come into God's presence and pour your heart out to Him. Are you concerned about how you will pay your next house note? Present your need to God in prayer. Are you anxious about the results of medical tests? Tell God how you feel. Thank Him for His continued faithfulness. Thank Him for His purposes for your life. Thank Him for how He is going to work. Give Him your need and receive His peace.

Reflect and Apply

What is the first thing you do when difficult circumstances arise? When do you turn to prayer?

List a few things you can praise and thank God for even in the midst of a desperate situation.

Recall a time God gave you peace in the middle of trouble. What was the situation?

Prayer Prompt

Spend a moment praising God for who He is and thanking Him for what He has done in your life.

Memory Minute

1. Recite 1 Peter 5:7 without looking at either the front or back of your card. If you can't get started, sneak a peek at your anchor words.
2. Write the verse out on another card to put in a prominent place. Review the verse whenever you see the card.
3. Now use your unique learning style to reinforce 1 Peter 5:7, such as making a recording, writing a song, developing hand motions, or assigning the verse to an object in your home.

4. Try to recite Psalm 139:14, Psalm 34:4, and Hebrews 12:14 from the fourth, fifth, and sixth weeks without looking at the cards. Use the anchor words on the back if you need help.

Day Five

At His Feet

Read: Luke 10:38–42
Weekly memory verse: 1 Peter 5:7

It happened to me every time I invited people over for dinner. The preparations consumed me. The menu had to be planned, and food had to be bought. The bathrooms had to be cleaned, and the shelves had to be dusted. I allowed the work to distract me from the reason for the evening, and I even took my frustrations out on my family. By the time it was over, I was exhausted. God asks us to practice hospitality, but I got off track. Not unlike Martha, I focused on the tasks rather than the people.

Martha served others and served them well. However, she allowed service to occupy the top of her priority list. She traded time *with* Jesus for time *serving* Jesus. Jesus calls us to serve Him and others, but service should be an outflow of our relationship with Him, not take the place of it. Martha's misplaced priorities created anxiety and worry. The details of "doing" consumed her, and the resulting frustration showed.

Marthas fill our churches. They make meals for grieving families and visit the sick. They welcome guests on Sunday mornings and serve at the soup kitchen on Thursdays. While the church and our community need to be served in these ways, too often we allow the busyness of service to overshadow our relationship with Jesus.

Mary made learning from Jesus her first priority. She found tranquility while her distracted sister worried about her long "to do" list. We must serve Jesus and others. But let's make time at the feet of Jesus our first priority. Then our service will be marked with peace and joy.

Reflect and Apply

Have you ever allowed the busyness of Christian service to draw you away from an intimate relationship with Jesus?

If so, how did you feel in the midst of serving? Fulfilled or frustrated? Anxious or peaceful?

How can you make time with Jesus your first priority?

Prayer Prompt

Ask God to show you if there is some area of service you need to step back from in order to spend more time with Him.

Memory Minute

1. Reflect on the truths in 1 Peter 5:7:
    a. How does God feel about you?

    b. How much of your trouble and worry can you bring to Him?

2. Recite 1 Peter 5:7 three times without looking at your card.
3. Try to recite Ephesians 3:20–21 and Matthew 11:28 from the seventh and eighth weeks without looking at the cards. Use the anchor words on the back if you need help.

WEEK TEN

TEMPTATION

Memory Verse

His divine power has given us everything we need for life and godliness through our knowledge of him who called us by his own glory and goodness.

2 Peter 1:3

Day One

Spiritual Bull's-Eye

Read: 2 Peter 1:1–4

Weekly memory verse: 2 Peter 1:3

On a dartboard, the bull's-eye—the small circle in the center—is the primary target. The goal is to throw the dart so it hits the target. Some players are more skilled at hitting the center than others, but even the best dart player cannot hit the bull's-eye every single time he throws a dart.

Christians have a goal, a target to hit. God's goal for us is Jesus (Rom. 8:29). Anytime our thoughts, attitudes, or behaviors do not accurately reflect those of Jesus, we sin. By definition, *sin* means to miss the true goal or target. Anything outside God's perfect will and everything not in keeping with God's holy character is sin.

Like me, you probably feel this target is impossible to hit. Our human nature and the world around us are both corrupted by sin. Left to our own inclinations, we will choose our own way over God's. We will fall when we rely on our own power to resist temptation. But, praise God, what He requires from us He also provides. God calls us to turn away from sin, and He also gives us the power we need to obey His call.

When Jesus saved us, He broke the hold of sin in our lives and gave us His Spirit. The Spirit's presence provides the power we need to resist our evil desires and embrace God's holiness. The Spirit helps us live lives that please God and reject the corruption of the world. When we choose to sin, we bring pain on ourselves and others around us. Instead, let's rely on God's divine power to experience the joy and freedom found in obedience.

Reflect and Apply

With what recurring sins do you struggle?

Use the truth found in 2 Peter 1:3 to write a statement about the power God has provided you to turn away from that sin. Be specific.

How can you rely on God's divine power to say no to that sin today?

Prayer Prompt

Ask God to help you recognize His power working in your life to choose godliness.

Memory Minute

Commit to memorize 2 Peter 1:3 to remind you that God has provided everything you need for godliness.

1. Read the verse in your favorite translation.
2. Rewrite the verse in your own words at the bottom of this page.
3. Write the verse and reference on a card for your memory system.
4. Read 2 Peter 1:3 out loud three times.

Day Two

Kick Off the High Heels

Read: Hebrews 12:1–3

Weekly memory verse: 2 Peter 1:3

A new rage in recent years is high heel races. Often, charities organize them as a fun and creative way to raise funds for their causes. A new twist on the traditional footrace, participants must run in high heels instead of running shoes. One event even offered suggestions for race preparation and safety. They gave advice like "strengthen your ankles" and "choose quality heels." However, it seems like the best advice would be "don't run in high heels!"

Most of the high-heeled runners can manage the hundred yards that most of these charity races require, but a marathon runner would never attempt the 26.2 miles on three-inch spikes. Running in high heels not only slows the runner's pace, but a fall or twisted ankle is also highly likely.

The author of Hebrews compares our life of faith to a long-distance race. To persevere in this race, we must get rid of anything that encumbers or holds us back. Unfortunately, like a marathon runner choosing to wear heels, we often try to follow Christ while hindered by sin that could trip us up.

Like the heroes of the faith who have gone before, let us rid our lives of anything that keeps us from complete obedience to Christ. Maybe a sinful habit or unhealthy relationship prevents us from fully submitting to our Savior. Perhaps pride or selfishness keeps us hanging onto our own will and way. Let's turn our full attention to Christ and consider what He endured for us. His example will help us throw off any sin that entangles us and run freely toward the finish line.

Reflect and Apply

Is there any activity in your life that holds you back from following Christ in complete obedience? If so, what is it?

Now consider your attitudes. What, if any, sinful attitudes or selfish motivations trip you up in your life of faith?

Imagine what your life of following Christ would be like without these activities and attitudes. Are you willing now to throw them off?

Prayer Prompt

Ask God to help you turn away from these things that hinder and entangle.

Memory Minute

1. Read 2 Peter 1:3 from the card you created yesterday.
2. Identify two to four anchor words in the verse to help you remember it. Circle these words on the front of the card and then write them on the back.
3. Recite the verse three times. The first time, read it from the card. The second time, check the anchor words on the front and then recite it. The third time, turn the card over and try to recite it by only looking at the anchor words.
4. Review your verses from the first weeks.

Day Three

Agreeing with God

Read: 1 John 1:8–10; 2:1–2
Weekly memory verse: 2 Peter 1:3

Americans have turned their backs on sin. No, we're not embracing repentance and holiness; we've simply decided to reject the *idea* of sin. Our western culture treats it like old-fashioned nonsense. "Sin" has been replaced with "freedom," "tolerance," and moral relativism. Even many popular Christian preachers admit their hesitation to use the word *sin* with their congregations because it might make someone feel bad.

However, ignoring sin does not make it go away any more than ignoring a cancerous mole makes it disappear. Sin is a spiritual reality with consequences in this life and the next. The cost of humanity's sinful condition was so high that only the sacrificial death of God's perfect Son could pay the price. When we refuse to acknowledge our sin, we also devalue Christ's sacrifice.

Our sinful human nature doesn't want to admit its sin. We pretend everything is okay and hope it will simply go away. Yet, the only way to receive God's forgiveness and move toward righteousness is confession. How ironic! The very thing we resist is the pathway to spiritual healing and growth.

Yes, we are all sinners. To claim otherwise is to call God a liar. But in His faithfulness, God has provided a way of forgiveness and a path to righteousness. Jesus Christ not only paid the price for our sin, He also stands before the Father and pleads our case before Him. Appeal to Jesus, your Savior and advocate. Agree with God and confess your sins to Him. He will faithfully forgive.

Reflect and Apply

What major discrepancies do you see between what society sees as sinful and what God identifies as sin?

Has our culture affected the way you view sin?

Are there any attitudes or behaviors in your life that society views as acceptable that God calls sin?

Prayer Prompt

Ask God to align your thinking with His and to help you recognize and turn away from sin.

Memory Minute

1. On the back of your 2 Peter 1:3 memory card, draw a symbol or picture that visually represents the verse.
2. Turn the card facedown so only the anchor words you wrote earlier and the picture you drew today can be seen. On a scratch sheet of paper, write out the verse with the reference. Refer to the anchor words and picture if you need help.
3. Now, without looking at either side of the card, recite the verse and reference from memory.
4. Review your verses from the fourth, fifth, and sixth weeks.

Day Four

Keep Your Guard Up

Read: 1 Corinthians 10:11–13
Weekly memory verse: 2 Peter 1:3

We did a lot of snow skiing during the years we lived near the mountains. Practice made me a decent skier, but I rarely pushed myself. I feared injury enough to be cautious. I shied away from black diamond slopes and worked to stay at a safe speed. These safety measures meant I didn't fall often. However, one particular time I let down my safety guard and discovered afresh the benefit of caution.

Skiers packed the mountain that bright afternoon. As I started down the slope, I noticed it ran underneath the chairlift all the way to the bottom. I could hear the skiers overhead talk to each other. Some commented on skiers on the ground. My pride took center stage. I threw caution to the wind, thinking I would dazzle the riders with my speed and grace. Instead, I entertained them with a spectacular end-over-end tumble. Thankfully, nothing was wounded but my pride.

I let down my guard and suffered the consequences—in front of a lot of people. I could have resisted the sin of pride, but I chose not to. Christians do not have to yield to temptation. God promises always to provide a way out. In his first letter to the Corinthian Christians, the Apostle Paul clearly writes about

God's faithfulness to give us the strength to resist. God will always show us how we can avoid yielding to sin.

Temptation is not sin, but yielding is. When we sin, it's because we have spurned God's strength and rejected His way of escape. Let's stay on guard against temptation and keep a diligent eye out for God's path of resistance.

Reflect and Apply

Think about the last time you yielded to temptation and sinned. (Maybe just this morning you snapped at a co-worker.) Describe the situation.

In retrospect, what could you have done to resist that temptation? What "way out" did you ignore?

Consider ways you can stand firm in the future. List some ways you can be on guard and watch for God's way of escape.

Prayer Prompt

Ask God to help you recognize the way out He provides when you are tempted. Thank Him for the strength He gives to resist.

Memory Minute

1. Recite 2 Peter 1:3 without looking at either the front or back of your card. If you can't get started, sneak a peek at your anchor words.
2. Write the verse out on another card to put in a prominent place. Review the verse whenever you see the card.

3. Now use your unique learning style to reinforce 2 Peter 1:3, such as making a recording, writing a song, developing hand motions, or assigning the verse to an object in your home.
4. Review the verses from the seventh, eighth, and ninth weeks.

Day Five

Recipe for Righteousness

Read: James 4:7–10
Weekly memory verse: 2 Peter 1:3

In the early 1970s, comedian Flip Wilson hosted a successful variety show. His popular character Geraldine coined a phrase that became her trademark. "The devil made me do it" even became a national expression, popping up on T-shirts and other items.

The phrase accurately reflects our human nature. We don't want to accept responsibility for our own sin. We prefer to blame someone else. Satan makes an easy target, since he does tempt us to turn away from God. But we Christians give Satan too much credit. He cannot make us sin. We just don't want to admit we are the problem.

Jesus' brother James wrote to Christians caught up in a cycle of sin. They had indulged their selfish desires and fallen into a myriad of sins. The result of their "friendship with the world" (James 4:4) was estrangement from God, their Father. But James had a remedy for their situation.

Pride was the root of their sin problem. Prideful people resist God. God resists the prideful, but God helps the humble. In today's passage, James gives ten commands for action that will lead Christians from prideful sin to humble obedience. These steps are a recipe for righteousness that begins with submitting our will to God's will. Although in this process grief accompanies true repentance, God promises to bring joy to those who humbly submit themselves to Him.

When we resist God, we invite the devil's temptations. But when we humbly submit ourselves to God, the devil has no power over us. The prideful sinfully resist God, but the humble successfully resist the devil. The devil *can't* make you do it!

Reflect and Apply

List all the verbs from today's reading that describe the actions Christians should take when they've chosen their own way over God's.

Why does grief accompany true repentance? Have you ever mourned your sin?

Why is humility a powerful weapon against the devil and his schemes?

Prayer Prompt

Ask God to show you areas of your life where pride has led you into sin.

Memory Minute

Use today as a review day. Try to recite all ten verses without looking at the cards. Use the key words only if you need them.

WEEK ELEVEN

GRIEF

Memory Verse

He will wipe every tear from their eyes. There will be no more death or mourning or crying or pain, for the old order of things has passed away.

Revelation 21:4

Day One

The New Order

Read: Revelation 21:1–4
Weekly memory verse: Revelation 21:4

Imagine a world without death or loss. A world without reason to mourn or grieve. A world without tears. But that is not the world we live in now. In this world, each of us will experience a multitude of losses. From the death of loved ones to the shattering of dreams, we will know many reasons to grieve. Many reasons to cry. This is the current order of things.

Before sin entered the world, no tears fell in the Garden. Before Adam and Eve chose their way over God's, no grief touched their hearts. Before disobedience marred Creation, death and pain left no mark. Then God's children ate from the forbidden tree and everything changed. The door opened to loss, grief entered, and tears have fallen ever since.

God did not create death, loss, and mourning when He created the world. They are products of a fallen world and thus temporary. When history is complete and Christ returns, God will once again set everything right. He will restore all things and reverse the effects of sin. God's full and permanent presence will eliminate all pain and suffering. There will be no more crying because there will no longer be any reason to cry.

When God makes His permanent dwelling with us, He will establish His new and eternal order. He will wipe away our tears and no more will fall. No grief. No pain. That will be the new order of things. Lord Jesus, come quickly.

Reflect and Apply

Think of the times you've cried—or felt like crying—in the last year. Briefly list the reasons for your tears.

In what ways has God worked to bring you comfort in these situations?

Now contemplate the glorious truth that one day God will forever remove all those reasons for grief.

Prayer Prompt

Write a brief prayer of thanksgiving to God that He will one day "wipe every tear" from your eye.

Memory Minute

Commit to memorize Revelation 21:4 as a comforting reminder that one day God will bring an end to grief.

1. Read the verse in your favorite translation.
2. Rewrite the verse in your own words at the bottom of this page.
3. Write the verse and reference on a card for your memory system.
4. Read Revelation 21:4 out loud three times.

Day Two

The Presence of the Comforter

Read: John 14:15–18
Weekly memory verse: Revelation 21:4

My friend Wende lost her son Ethan to a brain aneurysm when he was just nineteen. Ethan was diagnosed with Arteriovenous Malformation (AVM)—a rare, abnormal formation of blood vessels in the brain—when he was ten years old. AVM can cause seizures, hemorrhages, and strokes. Larger AVMs, like Ethan's, result in progressive neurological deterioration.

Not long after the diagnosis, Ethan suffered a stroke that left him with some physical challenges. Wende lovingly cared for Ethan and addressed the continuing health issues that resulted from the AVM. Although they lived daily with the possibility of a ruptured aneurysm, Wende kept the family going with strength and determination. Wende and her husband constantly worked to keep life as normal and happy as possible for Ethan and his two brothers.

For nine years, Wende grieved the loss of Ethan's health. Then Wende grieved an even greater loss—Ethan himself. How did she cope? Wende credits the constant comfort of the Holy Spirit. She recalls a specific moment days after the diagnosis: "I was washed by an overwhelming sense of God's peace and I felt God whisper, 'I've got this.' And I believed Him. From then on the Spirit gave me rest from all the things I had to deal with, so I could keep going."

On the night Jesus was arrested, He promised us the permanent, comforting presence of the Holy Spirit. Wende clung—and clings—to this promise and the comfort the Spirit gives. He pours peace into her life. He replaces sadness with joy and weakness with strength. The Holy Spirit's abiding presence is a constant reminder of God's love for Wende. He can be for you, too.

Reflect and Apply

The Holy Spirit lives within every true believer. "If anyone does not have the Spirit of Christ, he does not belong to Christ" (Rom. 8:9). Do you possess the indwelling presence of the Holy Spirit?

Recall times in the past you have felt the active presence of the Holy Spirit.

In what specific ways do you now need the comfort that only the Holy Spirit can provide?

Prayer Prompt

Bring these needs to the Spirit in prayer. Express your grief, sadness, and weakness. Ask Him to powerfully apply His presence to these areas.

Memory Minute

1. Read Revelation 21:4 from the card you created yesterday.
2. Identify two to four anchor words in the verse to help you remember it. Circle these words on the front of the card and then write them on the back.

3. Recite the verse three times. The first time, read it from the card. The second time, check the anchor words on the front and then recite it. The third time, turn the card over and try to recite it by only looking at the anchor words.

Day Three

Grieving with the Grieving

Read: 1 Corinthians 12:21–27
Weekly memory verse: Revelation 21:4

The day my mother-in-law died in a car accident, my husband and I experienced the comfort of the body of Christ. Immediately after we received the news, I called a friend from church to let her know. Within half an hour, our home began to fill up with members of our church family.

One friend spent two hours on the phone with the airline, making arrangements for us to fly from Calgary back home to Louisiana. Another set a time to pick us up and drive us to the airport. Another took the dog. Someone else planned to teach my husband's Sunday school class. Several more helped in other concrete and practical ways, but all of them grieved with us.

In a way that only God can accomplish, there's a unique sense of comfort when a fellow believer shares your grief. That night our church family prayed with us, wrapped their arms around us, and cried with us. Their presence did not remove our grief, but the joining of their hearts with ours gave us peace and strength. We were able to do what had to be done because they helped us carry the burden.

God designed the church this way. Every member of the body of Christ is spiritually linked to all the others. God uses each member to minister to the others. If you are connected to a local church, then you can experience the joy and comfort it provides. One believer's joy is all the members' joy. One believer's grief is all the members' grief. We rejoice together and we grieve together. And in the process, joy is multiplied and grief is eased.

Reflect and Apply

Since sin sometimes warps God's design for His church, let's remind ourselves what God intends. Look back through 1 Corinthians 12:21–27 and list the key truths about the body of Christ.

Are you currently actively involved with a local church? If not, why not?

If you are connected to a church, in what ways has God used the body to minister to you personally?

Prayer Prompt

Submit yourself to God as a ministry tool in your church. Ask Him to show you specific ways you can share joy and grief with the other members.

Memory Minute

Today is review day! Recite your verses from the first five weeks. Try to say them without looking at the cards. Use your anchor words only if necessary.

Day Four

For His Glory

Read: Isaiah 61:1–3
Weekly memory verse: Revelation 21:4

Yesterday, I passed a public building with an American flag displayed out front. When I noticed the flag flew at half-staff, I immediately wondered who had died. A flag at half-staff, along with black clothing and black armbands, is a visible sign of mourning. These acts outwardly express our inward feelings of grief.

People in biblical times also used outward signs to express their grief. For instance, when David's son Amnon raped his sister Tamar, she tore her robe and put ashes on her head in mourning. The presence of ashes clearly pointed to grief. God's people will grieve and outwardly express their grief. But as we saw in today's reading, our grief is an opportunity for God to display His glory to the world.

In Luke 4:21, Jesus boldly claimed to be the fulfillment of this prophecy in Isaiah 61. Yes, our hearts break, but Jesus, the Anointed One, will mend them. Yes, we face captivity, but Jesus will free us. Yes, we mourn, but Jesus will comfort us. When Jesus mends, frees, and comforts, our lives become a testimony to God's power and goodness. When Jesus cleans the ashes from our heads and lavishes us with the oil of gladness, our joy will point a watching world to God.

Jesus can change everything. Right now, you may feel like a weak sapling bent beneath the weight of grief. But when the Anointed One intervenes, He will relieve your burden and plant you in strength. You will be called an "oak of righteousness, a planting of the LORD for the display of his splendor." Your life will bring Him glory.

Reflect and Apply

Look back through Isaiah 61:1–3. Make two columns in your journal. On the left, list the negative circumstances we may face in this world. On the right, list the ways Jesus intervenes.

Think of a time God intervened in your life—or the life of someone close to you—and replaced your mourning with joy. Briefly describe it.

In what ways did that event point others to God? If you cannot remember any specific ways, brainstorm some ways you could have used the occasion to point others to Him.

Prayer Prompt

Ask God to show you how He wants to use the current circumstances of your life to bring Him glory.

Memory Minute

Today is the other half of our review for the week. Recite your verses from Weeks Six to Ten. Try to say them without looking at the cards. Use your anchor words only if necessary.

Day Five

Meanwhile, We Hope

Read: 1 Thessalonians 4:13–18
Weekly memory verse: Revelation 21:4

Last week, I visited the 9/11 Memorial at Ground Zero in Manhattan. The memorial is a beautiful tribute to the almost three thousand men and women who lost their lives on September 11, 2001, when terrorists attacked the twin towers of the World Trade Center. Two massive reflecting pools and waterfalls now occupy the spaces where the two towers once stood. The names of the victims are engraved on the ledges surrounding the pools. More than four hundred trees now grow in the plaza, dotting the landscape with life and growth.

A strong mix of emotions hit me as I walked the area. Anger, grief, patriotism, and hope each took its turn at the forefront of my feelings. So much loss. So many left to mourn. So many families torn apart. Yet even as our nation grieved, there was hope. Stories of courage, strength, and faith began to be told and shared, like the heroes of Flight 93 who gave their lives to save many others. When I visited the memorial, One World Trade Center—the new building being erected near the pools—was nearing completion. It will be the tallest building in America and a visual reminder of America's perseverance and commitment to freedom. We have grieved, but we move forward with hope.

Believers have a unique ability to grieve with hope. Yes, we experience loss, and we will mourn our loss. But, unlike those without Christ, we know our loss will be restored. When Christ returns, we will be united with those believers who have gone before us. Our loss is temporary. Our hope, eternal.

Reflect and Apply

Look back at 1 Thessalonians 4:13–18. What great promise does God make about our Christian loved ones who have died before us?

How does this promise make our grieving different than the rest of the world's grieving?

Think about someone you've lost. Apply God's promise and reflect on that hope!

Prayer Prompt

Pray for those around you who do not yet have a saving relationship with Christ. Ask God to draw them to Jesus.

Memory Minute

1. On the back of your Revelation 21:4 memory card, draw a symbol or picture that visually represents the verse.
2. Turn the card facedown so only the anchor words you wrote earlier and the picture you drew today can be seen. On a scratch sheet of paper, write out the verse with the reference. Refer to the anchor words and picture if you need help.
3. Now, without looking at either side of the card, recite the verse and reference.

WEEK TWELVE

DISCONTENTMENT

Memory Verse

For where your treasure is,
there your heart will be also.

Matthew 6:21

Day One

Where's Your Treasure?

Read: Matthew 6:19–21
Weekly memory verse: Matthew 6:21

Our family calls it the flood of 2003. One Saturday morning, I stepped into ankle-deep water in the hallway outside our bedroom. I could hear water gushing somewhere close-by and hurried to find the source. In the guest bathroom, water from the toilet supply line was shooting across the room. I turned off the water and began to survey the damage.

Carpets and other flooring upstairs were ruined. But the bigger mess was downstairs. The ceiling directly under the bathroom had fallen, and paint had slid down the walls. Water saturated everything in that half of the bottom floor of our house. We spent the rest of the summer repairing, replacing, and renovating.

The accident and the resulting damage to our home hit me hard. The physical challenge of the cleanup overwhelmed me, but I also grieved the loss of our stuff. Later on—when I was ready to hear it—God showed me my reaction to this material loss revealed much about what I treasured most.

In the Sermon on the Mount, Jesus addressed this very issue. He knows we humans tend to value the wrong things. We seek satisfaction, joy, and security in the fleeting things of this world. But jobs, possessions, money, and people cannot meet our deepest needs. They may temporarily mask our real need, but eventually discontentment rises to the surface again.

We've been taught by the world that "stuff" is the answer. So we stuff all we can into the empty hole, but it never fills up. Only God can fully and permanently satisfy our spiritual need. When He becomes what we value most, then we will find true contentment.

Reflect and Apply

Have you ever suffered a great material loss? How did you react? If you have never lost anything of material value, imagine for a moment how you would feel if a prized possession were stolen or destroyed.

What does your reaction reveal about where your heart is? Do you care too much about earthly things?

In what eternal things—like your relationship with God and the spiritual needs of other people—are you investing?

Prayer Prompt

Ask God to help you put the greatest investment in eternal things and to teach you how to hold earthly things with an open hand.

Memory Minute

Commit to memorize Matthew 6:21. Every time you recite it, do a quick heart check!

1. Read the verse in your favorite translation.

2. Rewrite the verse in your own words at the bottom of this page.
3. Write the verse and reference on a card for your memory system.
4. Read Matthew 6:21 out loud three times.

Day Two

Seeds of Greed

Read: 1 Timothy 6:6–10
Weekly memory verse: Matthew 6:21

Watch the nightly news for just a few moments and you will hear multiple reports of crimes motivated by greed. People rob banks, kidnap children, and even commit murder to fatten their wallets. Consider Bernard Madoff. In 2009, the seventy-one-year-old stockbroker was sentenced to 150 years in prison for securities fraud. Madoff reportedly lost fifty billion dollars of his investors' money in an elaborate Ponzi scheme. Madoff's "love of money" cost him his freedom.

The seeds of greed grow in the soil of discontent. Even law-abiding Christians can allow discontent to foster a desire for earthly things and alter their actions. We may not steal or kill in an attempt to satisfy our greed, but we may succumb to other kinds of harmful behavior. For instance, in an attempt to climb the corporate ladder, a parent may spend increasingly more time at work and less time with the family. A Christian salesman might embellish the description of his product to sell more items. I might fail to return a few dollars of extra change because I want to visit the Starbucks next door.

In our affluent culture, we often confuse true need with simple desire. Yes, we must have basic food, clothing, and shelter, but we don't *need* the latest cell phone. Something bigger, newer, brighter, or better will always come along. And when it does, discontent will be right on its heels.

Material gain and financial wealth will not bring us lasting contentment. That extra cash or afternoon coffee might yield some temporary pleasure, but nothing the world has to offer can add to our spiritual well-being. Only God can meet our soul needs.

Reflect and Apply

List any material things you feel you "need" right now. Honestly evaluate whether these things are true needs or simply desires.

Think about the last thing you got that you had been really wanting for a while. Did it meet your expectations? How long was it before you began to want something else?

Compare your pursuit of material things with your pursuit of God. On which of these do you spend the most time and energy?

Prayer Prompt

Ask God to reveal any actions and behaviors in your life motivated by desire for material gain. Repent and ask Him to give you a desire to pursue Him first.

Memory Minute

1. Read Matthew 6:21 from the card you created yesterday.
2. Identify two to four anchor words in the verse to help you remember it. Circle these words on the front of the card and then write them on the back.

3. Recite the verse three times. The first time, read it from the card. The second time, check the anchor words on the front and then recite it. The third time, turn the card over and try to recite it by only looking at the anchor words.

Day Three

Need Exceeded

Read: Luke 12:15–21
Weekly memory verse: Matthew 6:21

What do we need to be content? *Contentment*, as used in the New Testament, means a sufficiency of the necessities of life; satisfaction with what one has. Sufficiency plus satisfaction equals contentment. So why are we so often discontented?

The farmer in Jesus' parable was not content. He thought he needed bigger barns to store more. By the world's standards, he did the right thing. When work results in an abundant return, "wise" people invest it or save it for a rainy day. But how many barns must we build to secure a long and happy future?

Jesus did not fault the farmer for saving in general. Rather, Jesus denounced the man's attitude toward abundance. The farmer stored piles of grain and goods for himself, without considering how he could be generous with God. He selfishly hoarded earthly wealth and stingily withheld himself from his Creator. The farmer pursued possessions, but he failed to pursue his God.

Full, abundant life, the way God intends, cannot be found in material possessions (Luke 12:15). We cannot build enough barns to find contentment. True abundance can only be found in an intimate relationship with Christ. "I came that they may have life and have it abundantly" (John 10:10b ESV).

Abundance means to exceed the need. If we continue to seek contentment in the things of this world, we will remain needy. Discontentment will plague us. But if we invest our time, energy, and resources in our pursuit of Christ, we will experience the abundant life He promised. And Christ's abundance will surely exceed our need.

Reflect and Apply

Are your basic physical needs sufficiently met? Are you satisfied with these necessities, or are you discontented?

If you feel discontented, what do you think motivates these feelings?

In what ways do you actively pursue Christ? What do you do to deepen your relationship with Him?

Prayer Prompt

Ask God to shift your desire for material, earthly things to desire for Christ. Ask Him to fuel your passion for an intimate relationship with Him.

Memory Minute

Use today to review your first six verses. Try to recite each one without looking at the cards. Glance at your key words only if necessary. You are doing great!

Day Four

In Every Circumstance

Read: Philippians 4:10–13
Weekly memory verse: Matthew 6:21

Short-term mission trips have taken me to places very far and very different from North America. Two weeks after the coup of 1991, I went with a women's group to the former Soviet Union to distribute Bibles. In 2004, my husband and I, with others from our church, stayed in tents outside a village in Mozambique to drill a water well and show the Jesus film. I've journeyed twice to Moldova in Eastern Europe to encourage the church there and teach at a Bible seminary.

God taught me many things through these travels. For instance, one of the most important lessons I learned is that the body of Christ around the globe is beautiful and varied. Although we worship in different languages and styles, we all serve the same God.

I also learned Christians can be joyful and content without all the stuff we have in America. Believers in mud huts with dirt floors and thatched roofs ooze the joy of Christ. Brothers and sisters living in tiny Soviet block apartments experience the full life Christ gives.

In fact, I believe our material abundance can foster discontent. Since we are used to having so much, we have convinced ourselves we need it all. We trade in perfectly good cars for ones that are newer, brighter, or faster, and we upsize our homes even when we can't afford it.

The Apostle Paul could be content in material need or plenty because he did not base his attitude on his physical circumstances. Paul looked to Christ for strength in every situation, including physical need. The only thing Paul could not do without was Christ. I wonder: Can we say the same?

Reflect and Apply

How do your physical circumstances compare with the living conditions of a village in Mozambique?

In what ways, if any, has the material abundance of our culture fostered discontent in your own life?

Why can't material things bring lasting joy and contentment?

Prayer Prompt

Come before God and repent of any discontentment in your life. Be as specific as possible. Ask Him to replace your discontentment with contentment in Christ.

Memory Minute

Use today to review the five verses from the seventh through eleventh weeks. Try to recite each one without looking at the cards. Glance at your anchor words only if necessary. Keep up the good work. You're almost there!

Day Five

What Do You Long For?

Read: Psalm 63:1–5

Weekly memory verse: Matthew 6:21

Water is necessary to sustain physical life. Our bodies can survive for weeks without food, but they would succumb in only a few days without water. Making up about sixty percent of a healthy body, water lubricates the structures and provides shock protection for the organs. It regulates body temperature, aids in oxygen transportation, delivers nutrients to the tissues, and removes waste from the cells. Without enough water, the body cannot function.

If you've ever suffered from dehydration, you know how it feels to need water desperately. The body screams for what it needs to live. Until the body gets that life-sustaining liquid, nothing else matters. We fill a glass, grab a bottle out of the fridge, or stick our heads under the tap—whatever it takes.

Our souls need God like our bodies need water. He is the sole source of spiritual life. Yet, so often we stumble through life like we don't need Him. We look to anything and everything else in an attempt to satisfy the longings of our souls. But every time, we come up empty. Our thirst remains.

The psalmist David knew both physical and spiritual thirst. His time in the desert running from King Saul gave him the basis for the spiritual parallel we read today. Like a thirsty man longs for water, David's longing for God consumed him. As David turned to Him, God satisfied David's yearning with His love and constant presence.

The odd thing about experiencing God's love and presence is that complete satisfaction fosters deeper longing. Only God could create this beautiful spiritual paradox to keep His children close to Him. No matter our trial or difficulty, God's loving presence is our primary need. Draw close; drink deeply.

Reflect and Apply

Make a list of your spiritual needs.

God can fully and completely satisfy these needs. What should you do in light of this truth?

How can God's constant presence and love also help you in your physical need and difficult circumstances?

Prayer Prompt

David's reflection on God's provision in his life prompted praise. Spend a few moments today praising and honoring God.

Memory Minute

1. On the back of your Matthew 6:21 memory card, draw a symbol or picture that visually represents the verse.
2. Turn the card facedown so only the anchor words and the picture can be seen. On a scratch sheet of paper, write out the verse with the reference. Refer to the anchor words and picture if you need help.

3. Now, without looking at either side of the card, recite the verse and reference from memory.
4. Remember to continue to review all twelve verses on a regular basis so they stay imprinted on your heart and mind.

As I write this last devotion, I'm thinking about you. May God use this book to encourage your heart, strengthen your faith, and challenge your walk. Stay close to His side. He is your refuge and help.